THE CONTENT OF
SOCIAL EXPLANATION

THE CONTENT OF
SOCIAL EXPLANATION

SUSAN JAMES

FELLOW OF GIRTON COLLEGE, CAMBRIDGE

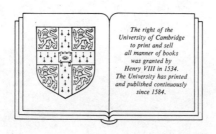

The right of the
University of Cambridge
to print and sell
all manner of books
was granted by
Henry VIII in 1534.
The University has printed
and published continuously
since 1584.

CAMBRIDGE UNIVERSITY PRESS

CAMBRIDGE

LONDON   NEW YORK   NEW ROCHELLE

MELBOURNE   SYDNEY

Published by the Press Syndicate of the University of Cambridge
The Pitt Building, Trumpington Street, Cambridge CB2 1RP
32 East 57th Street, New York, NY 10022, USA
296 Beaconsfield Parade, Middle Park, Melbourne 3206, Australia

First published 1984

Printed in Great Britain by the University Press, Cambridge

Library of Congress catalogue card number: 84-9632

British Library Cataloguing in Publication Data
James, Susan
The content of social explanation.
1. Social Sciences   2. Holism
I. Title
300'.1   H61
ISBN 0 521 26667 X

Contents

Acknowledgements

This book has taken me a long time to write, and it is a pleasure to thank all those who have helped with it. During the past few years I have talked about holist explanation with many different people whose reactions, positive and negative, have doubtless contributed more than I know to the following argument. I am grateful to them all for their time and attention, and hope that I have succeeded in taking their insights to heart.

In addition to these informal discussions I have also had the advantage of several sustained sets of comments. Of the individuals whose assistance has been crucial, my thanks are due first of all to the philosophers who read the Ph.D. thesis from which parts of Chapters i, ii and iv are drawn. My supervisor Mary Hesse, Richard Bernstein, Thomas Kuhn, Steven Lukes and Philip Pettit offered criticisms and suggestions which I have tried to accommodate. More recently, in writing the book itself, I have been helped by numerous friends and colleagues. The discussion of reduction in chapter I would have been more haphazard without the guidance of Nancy Maull, who shared with me her knowledge of the philosophy of biology. Chapter iii owes a great deal to the members of the philosophy department at the University of Connecticut; their responses to an earlier draft, particularly those of Joel Kupperman and John Troyer, enabled me to formulate the problem of holism more clearly. Anthony Giddens gave me some extremely helpful bibliographical advice. And part of Chapter iv was shaped by the criticisms of the History and Philosophy of Science seminar at the University of Cambridge. In addition, I have benefited from the expert typing of Mrs Anne Robson who patiently decoded a chaotic manuscript, and from the calm efficiency of Jeremy Mynott of the Cambridge University Press.

Most of all, however, I am grateful to the four people who

generously read the whole manuscript in its final stages of composition. The tenacious queries and suggestions raised by John Dunn, Raymond Geuss, Geoffrey Hawthorn and Quentin Skinner enabled me to revise several chapters, and I am deeply and contentedly indebted to them. Their thoughtful reflections on the problem of holism, as well as their steady encouragement, have been invaluable.

Finally, I should like to thank the Mistress and Fellows of Girton College, Cambridge for their support, and for the kindness and enthusiasm which make the college such a pleasant environment in which to work.

Introduction

This book is about two divergent types of social explanation, and the reasons that are given, and might be given, for favouring one approach over the other. One of the most startling features of the social world is its variety: the assortment of diets, laws, courtesies, kinship systems and rulers it contains is bound to strike us, and the things we should like to understand about it are correspondingly diverse, ranging from a fascination with the foibles of the Russian czars to a desire to empathise with the perception of the Other among the Boogys. But when we are not glorying in its eclecticism, our attempts to impose order on the social world continually hark back to the categories of the individual and society. Competing social theories embody incompatible conceptions of the relations between these two, and the terms themselves are characterised in all sorts of ways. Some of their features, however, are intuitively plain, such as the observation – usually taken for granted – that if a society is regarded as forming some sort of unit or whole, then individuals are among its parts. Individuals and societies stand in a particular relation to one another: that of parts to wholes. But the character and consequences of this apparently obvious connection have been the subject of a fierce and protracted debate, which still rages among social scientists and philosophers. In the following chapters I first analyse the arguments offered on both sides, and then show how they can be transcended, and the problem resolved.

The question of how individuals are related to the array of rules, institutions, roles and so forth – which for the moment can be called societies – gives rise to a view of social explanation known as holism. In the course of its recent history the term, amoeba-like, has sometimes encompassed a number of what were previously seen as distinct claims and has unified them into a single view, while at other times it has come to have a more restricted meaning,

as parts of the doctrine have split off again. Currently, I think it
is fair to say, there exist two separate and well-identified conceptions of what holism is, which bear very differently on the
part-whole relation between individuals and societies. The divide
between them is really less absolute than it is at first prone to appear
(a fact which accounts for their amoeboid cycle of development),
and in the course of this book some of the ways in which they
are connected will become plain. But before these links can be
appreciated, one must grasp the two views, each of which claims
that a particular kind of holist theory is better suited than its rival
to explaining the behaviour of individuals, societies, and the
relations between them.

Advocates of the first variety of holism, which I shall call *holism
of content*, are impressed by the way in which the characteristics
of social wholes are qualitatively distinct from the characteristics
of their parts.[1] Just as, for a student of animal behaviour, the
salient features of parrots are not those of their internal organs,
the properties of markets which interest many economists are not
those of individual buyers and sellers; and it is therefore natural
to ask whether such wholes as social groups can be satisfactorily
analysed and understood by means of theories which deal primarily
with their parts, or whether there is some discontinuity between
entities of the two types which makes such an approach either
impossible or inappropriate. Since societies just *are* collections of
individuals, surely the character of the whole must be explicable
as the outcome of its members' actions and dispositions. And yet
a society has an autonomy and history in the face of which
individuals sometimes seem powerless and insignificant. Of these
two views, both deeply-rooted in our intuitions, holists of
content defend the second, arguing that an adequate social theory

---

[1] This conviction gives rise to the doctrine of emergence, which I do not
discuss. See Gustave Bergmann, 'Holism, Historicism and Emergence',
Philosophy of Science 4 (1944) pp.209–21; A. Garnett, 'Scientific Method and
the Concept of Emergence', *Journal of Philosophy* 39 (1942) pp.477–86;
P. Henle, 'The Status of Emergence', *Journal of Philosophy* 39 (1942) pp.486–93;
M. Mandelbaum, 'Note on Emergence' in W. Baron, E. Nagel, K. Pinson
eds., *Freedom and Reason* (Glencoe, 1951) pp.175–83; J. Needham, *Time: The
Refreshing River* (London, 1943); M. Brodbeck, 'Methodological Individual-
ism: Definition and Reduction' in J. O'Neill ed. *Modes of Individualism and
Collectivism* (London, 1973) pp.287–311; K.-D. Opp, 'Group Size, Emergence
and Composition Laws: Are There Macroscopic Theories *sui generis*?', *The
Philosophy of the Social Sciences* 9 (1979) pp.445–55; and R. Bhaskar, *The
Possibility of Naturalism* (Brighton, 1979) pp.124–37.

must admit social wholes of some sort into its ontology, and that it will not prove possible to substitute for the explanations offered by such a theory explanations which do not appeal to the properties of wholes at all. Holism of content is therefore a general view about the *terms* of satisfactory social theories, but it can be defended on several grounds, some more respectful than others of the underlying part-whole distinction. On the one hand there are holists who believe that parts and wholes can be identified independently of one another, and that, as it happens, the properties of wholes yield more powerful explanations than do those of individual parts. This stand is usually accompanied by the further claim that theories about wholes are irreducible to theories about individuals so that an appeal to the whole is more than a convenience – it is an essential condition of understanding the social world.[2] On the other hand, there are holists who argue that the properties of individuals must be seen as a function of their place in societies. Their theories are necessarily holist as to content, in the sense that they appeal to the properties of wholes; but they attack the dichotomy between parts and wholes from which we began.[3]

This latter approach trenches on a second view, which I shall call *holism of form*. Unlike holism of content, holism of form does not concern the proper character of social theories. It is rather an account of the structure of theories, of the way in which their terms are related, and therefore applies quite generally to language, to the sciences, and to the mind, as well as to the social sciences. In itself this variety of holism constitutes a philosophical thesis which runs true to type in that it rests on a deceptively simple idea which is extremely difficult to spell out in detail.

Holism of form is a view about the relations between the terms of a theory: the view that each term owes its meaning to its relations with the others, so that they are all more or less closely interdefined, and a change in the meaning of one term will have repercussions for all the rest. Superficially this seems quite straightforward, but it has dramatic consequences for the way in which hypotheses are tested, consequences which are best appre-

---

[2] See Chapters II and III.

[3] See the discussion of Mandelbaum's position in Chapter III, and for a classic statement of this view, see F. H. Bradley, 'My Station and its Duties' in *Ethical Studies* 1st edition (London, 1876) p.158.

ciated by comparing holism of form to the empiricist approach, with which it can be sharply contrasted.[4] Suppose you want to know whether a particular hypothesis is true. According to the empiricist account, theories are deductively organised sets of laws and implications, and to test a hypothesis you have to see if it is supported by evidence independent of the theory. The available evidence is usually held to be of two sorts. First, there are observation statements, records of our perceptual experience which, because they are themselves untainted by theory, can be used to evaluate the truth or falsity of hypotheses. Second, there are analytic truths, propositions true by virtue of the meanings of their terms, which need no empirical confirmation. These are not used to test other claims directly, but they do restrict the range of propositions that can be admitted as true, for any true proposition must be consistent with them. Thus there are two fixed points from which to assess claims and find out their truth value: the world itself, and the meanings of terms. In both cases the process of testing is one of comparison: you find out if a claim corresponds to the facts, or you find out if it is consistent with pre-established analytical propositions.

Thoroughgoing holists of form deny that there are any facts or meanings which are not themselves 'theory-laden', and therefore repudiate this picture of the way theories are tested and built up.[5] Their rejection stems from the fundamental claim that the terms of theories are all interdefined, a claim which runs counter to the positivist distinction between theoretical claims and observation statements. For the meanings of even the most apparently observable terms such as 'square' or 'red' are said to derive not from their correspondence with a quality out there in the world, but from their place in theories which determine the criteria for squareness or redness. Thus our belief about whether or not a particular range of objects is red depends on other beliefs we hold, about, for example, the relation of light and colour, the spectrum, or the reliability of our senses.

Observation statements are therefore held to be not reflections

[4] For lucid accounts of this approach, see E. Nagel, *The Structure of Science* (London, 1961) Chapters III, IV, V, and C. Hempel, *The Philosophy of the Natural Sciences* (Englewood Cliffs, 1966).
[5] See P. Feyerabend, *Against Method* (London, 1978); T. Kuhn, *The Structure of Scientific Revolutions* (Chicago, 1962); M. Hesse, *The Structure of Scientific Inference* (London, 1974), Chapter I.

of reality, but, like other theoretical claims, interpretations of our experience offered in the light of our existing beliefs. And analytic truths suffer the same fate; for their meanings are not fixed once and for all.[6] The empiricist view of theories as made up of at least three different sorts of statements – analytic, theoretical and observation statements – is replaced by a more homogeneous analysis in which all statements get their meanings from their relations with the others, and none are immune from revision. The consequences for the traditional view of truth as correspondence are extremely serious. First, there is no independent standpoint from which to test claims; we must be content to rely on standards of evidence internal to theories themselves. Second, there is no neutral ground from which to compare theories, and we can only reject one from the standpoint of another.

The absence of any consensus about how to formulate this view in detail, how it applies to particular theories and what to do about it, gives holism of form a central position in current philosophy. Some of its advocates advise the undecided to lie back and enjoy it, give up the unrealisable quest for certainty, and recognise that standards of truth are a matter of social practice.[7] But it is more common to find philosophers puzzling over how to reconcile this view of the structure of theories with a conception of truth as a relation to the *world*.[8] And it is in this context that the term 'holism' is currently bandied about.

Holism of form is as much a feature of the social sciences as of anything else, and it has had a deep influence both on attempts to formulate theories in these disciplines and on efforts to understand those that already exist. The character of some of these projects will emerge in the course of this book. More important to the theme of holism in social theory, however, is the relation between the two kinds of holism I have identified – holism of form and holism of content. Because, in the history of philosophy, these

[6] See W. V. O. Quine, 'Two Dogmas of Empiricism' in *From a Logical Point of View* (Cambridge, Mass., 1953).
[7] See R. Rorty, *Philosophy and the Mirror of Nature* (Princeton, 1979); N. Goodman, *Ways of Worldmaking* (Hassocks, 1978).
[8] Defences of Realism are numerous. In the philosophy of language, see M. Dummett, 'What is a Theory of Meaning? (I)' in S. Guttenplan ed. *Mind and Language* (Oxford, 1975) pp.97–138 and 'What is a Theory of Meaning? (II)' in G. Evans and J. McDowell, eds. *Truth and Meaning* (Oxford, 1976); In the philosophy of science see J. Leplin ed. *Essays on Scientific Realism* (Notre Dame, 1983); W. H. Newton-Smith, *The Rationality of Science* (London, 1981).

have often been linked and sometimes fused, they are often
thought to be inseparable. But this is misleading, since the two
are in fact logically distinct; it is perfectly possible to conceive of
a theory which is holist as to form and individualist as to content,[9]
and equally possible to hold a view which allows theories that are
individualist in form yet holist in content. When philosophers of
language, or of science, discuss holism it is holism of form that
concerns them. But, perhaps surprisingly, this does not apply to
the social sciences. In this field, more than most, the question of
what kinds of theories it is possible or feasible to construct is so
open that 'the problem of holism', as it is known, is a problem
about holism of content: should social theories deal primarily with
individuals or with groups? Since the various suggestions that are
offered are based on conflicting evaluations of holism of form, the
latter cannot be completely ignored; but is not the main focus of
interest, and the following discussion will centre on holism of
content.

Once these two kinds of holism have been prised apart, it
becomes evident that some of the existing literature obscures an
already complex issue by conflating them. Even work which
focusses on holism of content, moreover, is frequently misleading.
For although it poses the question of how the terms of holist
theories are related to those of individualist ones, it does so in a
peculiarly rigid form which has given rise to a fruitless and
inconclusive debate. The problem of holism has usually been
identified with the question of whether theories about social
wholes can be *reduced* to those about individuals, and in the first
two chapters I begin by setting out this established approach. I
argue that it fails to resolve the problem it sets itself, and in
Chapter III go on to trace this deficiency to the fact that the
traditional debate mistakes the nature of the difference between
holists and individualists. By concentrating on the notion of
reduction, it misses a deeper and more important divide: holism
and individualism are based on competing views about the nature
of individuals, each of which gives rise to a distinctive account
of how to explain the social world. In the light of this insight the
problem can be seen afresh. Rather than having to do with the
various criteria for the reducibility of theories, it is concerned with
the relationship between, and comparative power of, two kinds

[9] See C. Peacocke, *Holistic Explanation* (Oxford, 1979).

of causal analysis: those that appeal to the properties of social wholes to account for features of individuals on the one hand, and those that seek to explain the characteristics of social wholes as the outcome of individual traits on the other.

Of these two views, individualism is the more intuitively familiar. Indeed, its hold over our imaginations is so strong that it is often regarded as invincible in the face of the holist challenge.[10] How, it is asked, could we give up our conception of ourselves as agents who can shake the world, and instead come to see individuals as pawns in the palm of society? The conviction that we could never make this transition, allied to a terror of the possibility that we might, has both strengthened the persuasiveness of individualism and given the problem of holism a certain shape. The individualist side of the argument has had the upper hand, and holism has been cast in a defensive role.

This bias may to some extent have drawn support from those analytical philosophers who have made the explanation of action the focus of their work. Like their colleagues in the social sciences, they tend to have individualist intuitions, and have thus favoured an individualist approach which links the understanding of action to a series of moral issues, of which the attribution of responsibility is the most prominent.[11] The sheer quantity of effort which has gone into this project, as well as the interest of its conclusions, have made it extremely influential. But its impact on the philosophy of the social sciences has not been altogether positive, and it has contributed to two unfortunate consequences.

First, the dominance of this approach has meant that individualist criteria for the explanation of action have come to be used in a manner that is merely stipulative. To cite the intentions, desires and so forth of individual agents is commonly regarded as *the* way to explain their actions,[12] so that holism, because it does not adopt these standards, is at once assumed to be inadequate.

[10] See Chapter III.
[11] See for example, H. L. A. Hart, 'The Ascription of Responsibility and Rights', *Proceedings of the Aristotelian Society* 49 (1948–9) pp.171–94; H. L. A. Hart and A. Honoré, *Causation and the Law* (Oxford, 1959); J. L. Austin, 'A Plea for Excuses' in *Philosophical Papers* (Oxford, 1961); J. Feinberg 'Action and Responsibility' in *The Philosophy of Action* ed. A. R. White (Oxford, 1968).
[12] Among distinguished exponents of this approach are E. Anscombe, *Intention* (Oxford, 1957); A. Kenny, *Action, Emotion and Will* (London, 1963); I. Melden, *Free Action* (London, 1961); D. Davidson, 'Actions, Reasons and Causes' in A. R. White, ed. *The Philosophy of Action*, pp.79–94.

If it is true, however, that the persuasiveness of individualism rests largely on its coincidence with our intuitions, to accept this view is to allow that social explanation is a fundamentally intuitive business. Never mind how the social world actually works, so long as we can hang on to our entrenched self-perceptions. But this is hardly satisfactory. Only by becoming aware of the assumptions implicit in individualism will we be able to adopt a more sceptical stance, one that will free us to ask why our intuitive sense of human character should be allowed to determine the nature of the theories we develop about the social world, and will thereby enable us to reconsider the merits of a holist approach. In Chapter III I therefore lay out those assumptions of individualism that stand in need of scrutiny, and identify an alternative set of holist premises, ripe for investigation.

As well as making individualism the norm, the mutual agreement between social theorists and philosophers as to how actions are to be explained falls foul of a second danger – that of cutting social theory off from whole areas of social science. When individualists want to show that their view is upheld in practice, they frequently turn to the models of rational choice used by economists.[13] But there are also sociologists, anthropologists and historians who do not espouse the underlying principle of individualism, and to broaden our understanding of the social world we must be receptive to the insights their work provides.[14] However, the existence of a strong consensus as to the superiority of individualism means that these tend to be discounted. Like any deeply entrenched view, individualism is inclined to be self-sustaining, and one of the costs of this has been the lack of much cross-fertilisation between the conclusions drawn by theorists and the views arrived at by practitioners. The second part of this book therefore aims to overcome the conventional impasse between holism and individualism by studying a range of holist explanations. In place of the well-worn strategy of finding out whether

---

[13] See J. Elster, 'Marxism, Functionalism and Game Theory: the Case for Methodological Individualism', *Theory and Society* 11 (1982) pp.453–82; G. A. Cohen, 'Reply to Elster on Marxism, Functionalism and Game Theory', *Theory and Society* 11 (1982) pp.483–95; J. Roemer, 'Methodological Individualism and Deductive Materialism', *Theory and Society* 11 (1982) pp.513–20; J. Berger and C. Offe, 'Functionalism and Rational Choice', *Theory and Society* 11 (1982) pp.521–6.

[14] See Part II.

the social sciences live up to standards set by philosophy, it aims to extract theory from practice – to learn from the social sciences themselves about the strengths and limits of holism.

As a means of highlighting the defining characteristics of a fully holist approach, Part II begins by investigating the theory that stands most unequivocally at one end of the spectrum of contemporary views about holism and individualism: the unqualified and unapologetically holistic theory of Louis Althusser. In Chapter iv, I explain the nature of Althusser's project, and point out some of the problems to which it gives rise. In Chapter v, I then take up the most important of the attempts which have been made to overcome these difficulties and thus to develop the Althusserean approach: an attempt embodied in the work of Nikos Poulantzas.

I argue that these theories, deeply suggestive though they are, remain open to extremely serious objections. My first general conclusion, therefore, is that, in the form in which it has been most ambitiously presented in contemporary social philosophy, a fully holistic account of social explanation does not succeed. This does not, however, leave individualism in possession of the stage. On the contrary, I devote my last chapter to elaborating a more concessive form of holism, one that is capable of taking account of the criticisms levelled at a fully holistic approach, without sliding back into endorsing an individualist point of view. Holism and individualism, I argue, must be seen as separate explanatory projects, each guided by an underlying *interest* in relation to which questions are asked and theories assessed. This interpretation undercuts the claim that there is an *a priori* case in favour of individualism, thus recasting the problem of holism as a dispute between equal parties, and at the same time suggesting a way of resolving the problem by adopting a pragmatic and explicitly normative account of social explanation. The main conclusion of this study is that this form of concessive holism in fact represents a more fruitful approach to social explanation than its rivals, and thus that individualism must relinquish its current hegemony.

PART I

Theory: two views of holism

I

The legacy of
analytical philosophy

During the past decade, the long drawn out discussion between holists and individualists in the philosophy of the social sciences has become notorious for its lack of progress. Despite the fact that the question it addresses is commonly acknowledged to be of great importance, the debate itself is frequently condemned as sterile, trivial or misguided, and few efforts have been made to overcome this unhappy state of intellectual affairs. Respect for the problem continues to be accompanied by disdain for the proposed solutions. Yet the issue of holism *versus* individualism, if it is significant, deserves to be dealt with in terms that do not excite contempt, and therefore needs to be liberated from the narrow circle of argument within which it has become confined. One of the aims of this book is to show that much of the current discussion is rooted in a small number of competing premises which control the goals and the modes of argument used by both sides. Because these are rarely made explicit, the true characteristics of both holism of content and individualism tend to be obscured, and their place in the broader field of the philosophy of the social sciences is misunderstood. To understand how the problem acquired its present shape and why it persists, these assumptions must be brought to light. And once we are able to examine them it will prove possible to recast the dispute in a new and more arresting form.

In the course of this chapter I shall argue that the prevailing approach to the problem of holism owes a good deal to some of the more rigid doctrines associated with analytical philosophy. The main body of literature regards the question of whether the explanatory power of theories about social wholes can be matched or outstripped by that of theories about individuals as equivalent to the question of whether theories of the first type can be *reduced* to those of the second.[1] Reduction therefore holds the stage, and any queries or insights that it cannot accommodate are left hovering in the wings or are cut out of the play altogether. After briefly explaining the issue as it appears from this standpoint I shall offer an account of the philosophical presumptions which make this approach seem so compelling. Then, in the remaining sections of the chapter, I shall consider the character of the relation of reduction.

The notion of reduction appealed to by holists and individualists alike has mainly been developed in the context of the physical sciences. In these disciplines – each containing a number of powerful and relatively discrete theories with their own subject matters and their own laws – it has seemed natural to ask how theories are connected to one another. Can we, for example, establish a link between mechanics and thermodynamics? What is the relation between classical and quantum mechanics? In the course of studying such questions, scientists and philosophers have isolated several kinds of connection, reduction among them. The basic character of this relation is straightforward and easy to grasp. Imagine a pair of discrete theories T_1 and T_2; for T_2 to be reduced to T_1 it must be shown that the first theory is a special case of the second. While the two had previously been regarded as separate, reduction shows that T_1 is sufficiently powerful to explain the phenomena dealt with by both, and it does this by demonstrating that the laws of T_2 can be *deduced* from those of T_1.[2]

Ever since this basic account of reduction was proposed, it has been embellished and refined as philosophy has broken the clean, Bauhaus lines of positivism with the exuberant decoration of post-empiricism. But the root conception has not changed, and

---

[1] See, for example, the following discussions: Robert Brown, *Rules and Laws in Sociology* (London, 1973), p.137; Maurice Mandelbaum, 'Societal Facts' in J. O'Neill ed. *Modes of Individualism and Collectivism* (London, 1973) pp.221–54; D. H. Mellor, 'The Reduction of Society', *Philosophy* 57 (1982) pp.51–75; Vernon Pratt, *The Philosophy of the Social Sciences* (London, 1977) pp.108–10; Martin Bridgstock and Michael Hyland, 'Reductionism: Comments on Some Recent Work', *Philosophy of the Social Sciences* 4 (1974) pp.197–200; David-Hillel Ruben, 'The Existence of Social Entities', *Philosophical Quarterly* 32 (1982) pp.295–310; R. Nozick, 'On Austrian Methodology', *Synthese* 36 (1977) pp.353–92; W. Block, 'On Nozick's "On Austrian Methodology"', *Inquiry* 23 (1980) pp.397–444.
[2] For the standard account of heterogeneous reduction, see Ernest Nagel, *The Structure of Science* (London, 1961) ch. XI.

is applied to the social as much as to the physical sciences, so that to ask whether a particular theory about social wholes can be reduced to one about individuals is to start off by asking whether this deductive relation can be established.[3] Both the individualist claim that it always can, and the holist claim that it sometimes cannot, are indebted to a collection of insights and impasses inherited from the philosophy of science: on the one hand they have borrowed a sophisticated definition of reduction, and on the other have been forearmed with the knowledge that it tends to break down and proliferate as soon as it is applied to particular examples.

Before going on to discuss this issue, let us spell out the idea of reduction in a little more detail. The simplest analysis of the relation assumed that T1 contains terms a_1, b_1... and laws such as $(x)(a_1 x \supset b_1 x)$, $(x)(c_1 x \supset a_1 x)$, and so on. Similarly, T2 has terms a_2, b_2..., and laws stating connections between them. The reduction of T2 to T1 is then made up of two steps. The first, known as the condition of connectability, states that the terms of the two theories must be linked by 'bridge laws' or 'reduction functions' of the form

$$(x)(a_2 x \supset a_1 x)$$

$$(x)(b_1 x \supset b_2 x)$$

The second, known as the condition of derivability, requires that the laws of T2 should be *deduced* from those of T1. For example, with the help of the above bridge laws we can deduce the law of T2, $(x)(a_2 x \supset b_2 x)$ from the law of T1, $(x)(a_1 x \supset b_1 x)$.[4]

From the standpoint of traditional philosophy of science, it is perfectly reasonable to ask whether this relation, which has enlarged our grasp of physics, can be applied to social theories. Rather as thermodynamics proved to be reducible to statistical mechanics, might not a particular theory about social wholes be reducible to one about individuals? And would not this discovery give us a richer understanding of the social world? The answer to this question is then regarded as giving the solution to the problem of holism: if the answer is positive individualism triumphs, while if it is negative holism is vindicated. This strategy

---

[3] See, for example, Mellor, 'The Reduction of Society'; Bridgstock and Hyland, 'Reductionism: Comments on Some Recent Work'.

[4] See Nagel, *The Structure of Science*.

is puzzling, however, for it is not at all obvious that the problem can be resolved along these lines. As we saw earlier, it concerns the comparative explanatory power of two types of theories, which have so far been differentiated as those about social wholes and those about individuals. It is true, of course, that their explanatory potentials *may* be revealed by the discovery that theories of one type are reducible to those of another. But there may also be other methods of assessing explanatory power, and thus of approaching the problem of holism, which are neglected when attention is focussed too narrowly on reduction.

In the following chapters, I shall argue that the issue of reduction is indeed tangential to the problem of holism, and that the standard identification of the two is a mistake. To find this conclusion compelling, however, one must understand what is wrong with the individualist view that theories about social wholes are reducible, and I shall aim to show that it is inadequate in two different ways, one more analytic, the other more historical. In Chapter II I shall take the arguments for the reducibility of social wholes on their own terms, and show that they are weak: they are incomplete, appeal to unexamined assumptions and assume their own conclusions. But first, I shall defend the interpretatively more complex thesis that the equation of the issue of holism with that of reducibility is rooted in various suspect presuppositions of logical positivism from which the problem of holism has never entirely been freed. If we pause to ask what general outlook on the social sciences and the nature of explanation made it clear that the problem of holism was to be resolved by way of reduction, we are drawn back to some of the cruder claims made by positivist philosophers of science, and to the role they have played in upholding individualism.

These views have, of course, been generally superseded, but they are nevertheless of great importance in understanding the holist debate on two separate counts. First, since they are still tacitly adhered to by a number of writers, an awareness of them suggests ways of unravelling knots in the contemporary literature. Second, and much more significant, a grasp of the positivist account of reduction casts light on the post-positivist treatment of the subject, and reveals it as a survivor from an earlier epoch. By starting with a discussion of some aspects of logical positivism, one can rebuild a framework within which individualism appeared highly plausible, and from which it still draws much of its support. This basis will then serve to illuminate the subsequent development of the debate.

The individualist belief that theories about social wholes are reducible to those about individuals can, I have suggested, be traced to a number of doctrines associated with logical positivism, which have often been misunderstood or misappropriated by philosophers of social science. Their influence can be discerned even in the work of people who would, if asked, energetically reject them, and they play a part in shaping both the questions that are posed and the terms in which they are answered. Positivism thus continues to overshadow the debate between holists and individualists to a degree that is by now singular and intriguing. To substantiate this claim, inferred more from the spirit than the letter of the recent literature, I shall discuss two features of logical positivism – its plea for the unification of science and its theory of meaning – and show that both are still being used in defence of individualism, despite their jaded reputation. A discussion of these ill-founded assumptions will thus help to reveal both the character of individualism and the motive for espousing it.

The connection between reduction and the doctrine of unification is quite explicit. The suggestion that the various scientific disciplines could be unified into a single science drew its strength from the belief that they all share one method and one source of knowledge, one mode of explanation and one kind of subject matter, so that the jumble of terms employed in biology, psychology, mineralogy and the like could be replaced by a universal language in which all laws were expressed. This aspiration, which mutated rapidly throughout the 1930s and 1940s, was forcefully presented by Carnap in 1931. Discussing the case of biology, he wrote,

Biological determinations involve such notions as species, organisms and organs, events in entire organisms or in parts of such organisms, etc.... Such notions are always defined by means of certain perceptible criteria, i.e. qualitative determinations capable of being physicalised; e.g. 'fertilisation' is defined as the union of spermatozoon and egg; 'spermatozoon' and 'egg' are defined as cells of specified origin and specified perceptible properties; 'union' as an event consisting of a specific redistribution of parts, etc...The same is true in general of all biological determinations, whose definitions always supply empirical and perceptible criteria...

The preceding argument shows that every statement in biology can be translated into physical language. This is true, in the first instance, of singular statements concerning isolated events; the corresponding result for biological laws follows immediately. For a natural law is no more than a general formula used for deriving singular statements from other singular statements. Hence, no natural law in any field can contain determinations absent from the singular statements in the same field.[5]

In this early work, Carnap conceived the universal language of science as that of physics, and boldly drew the conclusion that, 'Because the physical language is the language of Science, the whole of Science becomes physics.'[6] Later he adopted the different view that the basis of a unified science is not physics after all, but an observation language which records what have since been called 'raw feels' – our uninterpreted sensory perceptions.[7] In both versions, however, one language is held to be more fundamental than the rest, in the sense that others can be translated into it; the project of unification then consists in making more and more translations. The place of reduction in this enterprise is now perfectly clear: if theories could be reduced, and in the process rendered superfluous, fewer would remain to be unified.

This grand scheme has had a pervasive effect on the philosophy of the social sciences. First, the association of reduction with the unification of scientific theories helps to tip the scales of intuition in favour of individualism. If it is assumed that there are no qualitative discontinuities between theories, and if social wholes are collections of individuals, then it is on the face of things reasonable to expect that social wholes will be reducible. The problem of holism then consists not so much in *whether* this is so, but in how it can be *shown* to be so; and the holist position, by virtue of the way it is defined, is allotted a defensive role. The assumptions that give rise to this framework thus give the problem a certain shape, which is sustained by the more detailed exposition of the idea of unification. For the positivist view of the relation between physics and the other disciplines, which Carnap presents so clearly, often serves as a tacit model for the relation

[5] Rudolf Carnap, *The Unity of Science* (London, 1934), pp.69–71.
[6] *Ibid.*, pp.97–8.
[7] Rudolf Carnap, 'The Old and the New Logic', in A. Ayer ed. *Logical Positivism* (New York, 1959) pp.143–4.

between theories about individuals and theories about social wholes, an unspoken comparison that casts light on several aspects of the debate over reducibility. Most obviously, explanations offered in individualist terms tend to be regarded, like those of physics, or indeed like those of the observation language, as more basic than those which cite social wholes. As one writer puts it, they are 'rock-bottom' explanations which, by getting to the root of the subject-matter, offer a firmer grasp of the workings of society than their holistic analogues.[8]

These judgments, insofar as they are sustained at all, rest on the ontological intuition that parts are prior to wholes, together with the belief that statements about individuals can be more reliably tested than those about social wholes. Later I shall offer reasons for doubting the alleged conclusiveness of these claims. Meanwhile, it is not difficult to see that the analogy between the universal language of science (whether physics or a special observation language) on the one hand, and individualism on the other, is exceedingly weak. For one thing, Carnap envisaged the unification of *all* sciences, including the sciences of society, and would not have relished the dichotomy implied in the suggestion that, just as the language of physics is fundamental to the natural sciences, so the language of individualism is the key to the social ones.[9] And there are in addition other striking dissimilarities to consider. First, social scientists cannot boast a coherent body of theory as physicists can, and are thus not in a position to show that individualist theories provide powerful and fruitful explanations. Second, there is no social analogue of the view that theories of physics deal with the smallest components of matter. Individuals are, it is true, among the components of social wholes. But in explaining social life why should we not move on down, so to speak, to a physiological or electro-chemical level?

The moral of these asymmetries can be quickly drawn: unlike

[8] See M. Lessnoff, *The Structure of Social Science* (London, 1975); J. W. N. Watkins, 'Historical Explanation in the Social Sciences' in O'Neill ed., *Modes of Individualism and Collectivism*, p.168. For cogent criticism of this view, see Carl Hempel, 'Implications of Carnap's work for the Philosophy of Science' in P. A. Schilpp ed. *The Philosophy of Rudolf Carnap*, (La Salle, Illinois, 1963) p.702.

[9] Rudolf Carnap, *The Unity of Science*, p.96; 'The Old and the New Logic', p.144. See also Paul Oppenheim and Hilary Putnam, 'The Unity of Science as a Working Hypothesis' in H. Feigl, M. Scriven and G. Maxwell, eds. *Concepts, Theories and the Mind-Body Problem, Minnesota Studies in the Philosophy of Science* vol. II (Minneapolis, 1968) pp.3–36.

the selection of terms used in physical theories, the insistence that individuals must be the basic units of social explanations is an arbitrary one. Individualism derives its initial plausibility from its claim to be able to explain both the behaviour of individuals and that of social wholes. But while no one denies that individuals are among the physical components of groups, institutions, structures and so forth – and in this sense are part of wholes – it remains to be shown that social wholes can be *explained* if they are viewed as collections of individuals. Settling this question one way or the other is more complicated than many individualists seem to realise, and is not resolved by the plain observation that there is a part-whole relation between individuals and groups, nor by a comparison of individualism and the observation language.

Nevertheless, the projects of reduction and unification are often mistakenly identified, and lackadaisical attempts to turn the first into the second have generated a series of prejudices and misunderstandings. The claim that theories about social wholes can be *reduced* to theories about individuals has recently been defended, for example, by an appeal to an argument which is exactly analogous to Carnap's case for the unification of biology and physics. Any statement about social wholes, it is claimed, can be translated into a statement about individuals, and it follows that the laws of theories about social wholes can be expressed in individualist terms.

If every statement about a social object is equivalent to, and can be replaced by, a statement in which the predicates, whether the same or different as in the original statement, are predicates of individuals, then it rather trivially follows that every law about social objects is derivable from a law about individuals, since it must implicitly be such a law itself.[10]

So all explanations that cite social wholes and their properties can simply be replaced by ones that appeal to individuals.

Quite apart from the question of whether or not there is any reason to believe this claim, it is important to distinguish it from the view that theories about social wholes can be *reduced* to theories about individuals; for, as Carnap himself was quick to point out, when we 'translate' the laws of theories of the former type into the language of individualism, there is no guarantee that we shall end up with the laws of any existing theory about individuals, rather than just with a collection of individual statements.[11] The fact that the argument I have just quoted is offered as a defence of the reducibility of social wholes, and thus as a defence of methodological individualism, reveals two widespread and closely connected misconceptions. First, it confuses unification with reduction, by supposing that the latter is a matter of translating predicates rather than of establishing a particular logical relation between the laws of theories.[12] Second, it assumes that the requirements of individualism are met whenever we use statements that contain only individual predicates, regardless of their relations or explanatory power. There is thus a tendency to define individualism as any old bunch of *ad hoc* statements about individuals, and to forget that what is needed are *theories* of individual behaviour.[13]

The positivist doctrine of the unification of science has therefore left an enduring mark on the debate between holists and individualists, both in the straightforward sense that it has been, and continues to be, conflated with the notion of reduction, and in the more subtle fashion in which its assumptions render individualism plausible. I shall now suggest that the theory of meaning associated with logical positivism, and in particular the conception of a theory-free observation language, have been equally influential. In fact, one of the standard arguments for individualism starts with the assumption that statements about individuals themselves belong to the observation-language. The argument then comes in two parts, the first of which claims that statements about social wholes can only be tested by means of statements about individuals. For example, a sentence such as 'The CIA is powerful' cannot be verified directly: rather it must be broken up into a number of individual claims – 'The Director exerts influence over the President', 'The chief agent in Bogota is blackmailing the Minister for Foreign Affairs', 'An agent in Hawaii has just concluded an advantageous arms deal', and so

[11] R. Carnap, 'Logical Foundations of the Unity of Science', in O. Neurath, R. Carnap, C. Morris, eds., *International Encyclopaedia of Unified Science* vol. 1 (Chicago, 1955) pp.60–2.
[12] Quinton, 'Social Objects', pp.23–7.
[13] See, for example, K. Popper, *The Poverty of Historicism* (London, 1957) pp.135–6; F. A. Hayek, *The Counter Revolution of Science* (New York, 1964) pp.54–5.

on – which can then be tested. If they turn out to be true we can conclude that the CIA is powerful, but if not, not. This view is in turn justified by appealing to the second important implication of the supposed correlation between individual and observable statements, and between social and theoretical ones; for in addition to providing a means of testing statements about social wholes, individual predicates are said to supply their *meanings*. Thus, we can discover whether the CIA is powerful once we know the truth value of a number of individual statements such as those in the example, for the simple reason that their being true is what it *is* for the organisation to be powerful. That is what the sentence *means*.

Although the positivist theory of meaning has in general been abandoned, expositions and defences of this view, such as the one below are everywhere to be found in the current debate between holists and individualists. Just as the idea of individuals as the basic units of explanation is used to license a presupposition of reducibility, so the equation of individualism and the observation-language gives rise to a further argument.

It can scarcely be denied that any social description implies the truth of several (often many) individual descriptions... for otherwise it would be impossible to test social statements by observation and there could be no social science. But in that case, the anti-individualist position must assert that social descriptions mean *more* than can be reproduced by the meaning of the individual descriptions. This has the following very strange implication. The meaning of a statement such as 'British society is oligarchic' must be divisible into two parts, one which can be translated into statements describing the behaviour and attitudes of individuals and is observationally testable, while the other is not so translatable and testable. Let us suppose that the entire testable portion of this statement is translated, tested, and found to be true. Does it then follow that British society is oligarchic? On the anti-individualist position, no – for 'British society is oligarchic' means more than its partial, testable translation. It is, on this view, perfectly possible that although all the individual manifestations of oligarchy are present in a society, nevertheless that society is not oligarchic.[14]

The view that individual predicates supply both the meanings and the means of testing social predicates is supposed to show that sentences about social wholes must, taken on their own, be both

[14] M. Lessnoff, *The Structure of Social Science*, pp.80–1.

unverifiable and incomprehensible. Here, the claim that they are as a matter of fact translatable into statements about individuals is strengthened into the claim that they *must* be translatable if they are to make any sense, a change which alters the terms of the debate. For rather than allowing that there are theories about social wholes and theories about individuals, and then examining the relation between them, this approach undermines the assumption that there are viable social theories in social science. It therefore implies that the issue of reduction can be bypassed, and that individualism vanquishes holism by default.

Perhaps not surprisingly, this view is vulnerable to two objections, a minor one responding to the claim that statements about social wholes can only be tested by statements about individuals, and a major one aimed at the suggestion that individual predicates give meaning to social ones. The first is rooted in the simple observation that some predicates applied to social wholes are observable; for example, we can watch a posse of policemen charging at a crowd, or a team of removal men lifting a piano. The difficulty of drawing a distinction between the observable and theoretical (and, for that matter, between the individual and the social) makes such cases highly contentious. But we can at least say that, if there are any observable predicates, then some of them are social; and if this is so the individualist will have to concede that some social statements can be tested without the mediation of individual ones. At this point, defenders of individualism may allow that such predicates exist, but claim that they are too few to threaten the hegemony of individualist theories. And if this were the only criticism of their view, it might conceivably survive intact. But the second objection, which focusses on the claim that individual predicates give meaning to social predicates, cuts more deeply, and undermines both the theory of meaning and the method of verification on which this defence of individualism is founded.

The simplest aspect of this objection consists in the point that the reduction sentences used to translate theoretical predicates into the observation language do not provide complete definitions of the predicates concerned. They do not give their meanings, and at best give partial definitions. So even if it proved possible to translate social predicates into individual ones in the manner just discussed, this would not (or not necessarily) give us the meanings of those social predicates. However, still more serious than this allegation is the attack on the very distinction between observable and theoretical terms (and hence between an observation language and a number of theories) which was outlined in the Introduction. For this suggests that, even if the observation content of individual predicates is characteristically much higher than that of social ones, it does not follow that social predicates must be defined by their relationships to the observable characteristics of individuals. Instead, their meanings will be given by the laws and generalisations of the theories of which they are parts, which will relate them to predicates with both more and less observation content. And it is then possible that a social predicate may be primarily defined by its relations to other social predicates, without thereby becoming nonsensical.[15]

Some current defences of individualism, I have suggested, draw their strength from a logical positivism long since abandoned by most analytical philosophers; and objections to the assumptions on which they are based undermine the arguments themselves. If the reductionist approach to the problem of holism is to merit further discussion, the debate must be conducted in terms which are not tainted by unacceptable features of positivism. We therefore need to look in more detail at the most refined of the available conceptions of reduction, in order to see exactly in what the disagreement between holists and individualists now consists.

The canonical account of reduction focusses, as we have seen, on the task of deducing the laws of one theory from those of another.[16] But the attractions of the approach, and the felicity of fixing on a deductive relation between theories, derive from a general view of what reduction is supposed to achieve. To start with a straightforward point, since the process of reducing one theory to another is supposed to demonstrate the broader scope of the reducing theory, the relation has to be asymmetrical, and deducibility satisfies this condition nicely: the laws of T_1 can be deduced from those of T_2, but not *vice versa*. The same could be said, however, of a variety of other relations, and the choice of this particular one is due to the belief that reduction is a means

---

[15] For this view, see M. Hesse, *The Structure of Scientific Inference* (London, 1974) ch. 1, secn. 2; N. R. Hanson, *Patterns of Discovery* (Cambridge, 1958) ch. 1; T. S. Kuhn, *The Structure of Scientific Revolutions* (Chicago, 1962).

[16] See E. Nagel, *The Structure of Science*, ch. XI.

of explanation. Reducing one theory to another is not simply an exercise in the use of the predicate calculus, intended to reveal the relations between two sets of laws. It is at the same time a way of illuminating the character of the reduced theory, and revealing the hitherto unsuspected power of the reducing one. For the latter proves broader in scope than its rival, which can therefore be subsumed under it. In rare cases this process may render the reduced theory dispensable, for it may prove advantageous to use the reducing theory wherever the reduced one held sway. But more often the reduced theory continues to be used in at least some contexts on grounds of convenience, simplicity or the like, and reduction serves as much to increase our understanding of a science as to alter its practice. The reduction of thermodynamics to statistical mechanics, for example, did not herald the end of the first theory, though it did explain a great deal about the relation of the two.[17]

For the original defenders of Nagel's account the coincidence of reduction and deducibility was a natural one. Their belief that reduction should be explanatory led them to select deduction as the salient relation between the laws of theories, since they also espoused the so-called hypothetico-deductive model of explanation: the view that explanation always consists in deducing the proposition that is to be explained from a collection of laws and antecedent conditions. Advocates of this model therefore began with the established belief that explanations are deductive, added the requirement that reduction should be explanatory, and were able to draw the conclusion that reduction must be deductive too.[18]

Since it was first proposed, this traditional account of reduction has been much criticised. But it remains the usual starting-point for discussions of the subject, and is constantly referred to as an analysis that demands to be accommodated or rebutted. Of the numerous objections voiced against it, many seek to modify it or restrict its application and thus present only a limited threat.[19]

---

[17] *Ibid.*, pp.338–45.
[18] See, for example, C. Hempel, *Aspects of Scientific Explanation* (New York, 1965) pp.245–90.
[19] See Nancy Maull, 'Unifying Science without Reduction', *Studies in the History and Philosophy of Science* 8 (1977) pp.143–62; Thomas Nickles, 'Two Concepts of Intertheoretic Reduction', *The Journal of Philosophy* 70 (1973) pp.181–201; Lawrence Sklar, 'Types of Intertheoretic Reduction', *British Journal of the Philosophy of Science* 18 (1967) pp.109–24.

Others, however, aim to oust it altogether, and since they usually proceed from different premises, can only be assessed in the light of further philosophical conclusions.[20] The hypothetico-deductive model of explanation, for example, which provided a powerful reason for thinking that deducibility was an essential feature of reduction, has since come under heavy attack, both on the grounds that not all explanations are deductive, and on the ground that some deductions are not explanatory.[21] Succeeding and more pluralist models of explanation have given rise to the suggestion that deduction may not be an integral part of reduction after all; but here the two issues of explanation and reduction have to be judged together.[22] Criticisms of the standard view are thus of two types (those designed to modify it and those aimed at dispensing with it altogether), which require to be treated in rather different ways. Both, however, tend to focus on the analysis of the first step in the process of reduction – the condition of connectability – which therefore forms the fulcrum of the argument.

The condition of connectability, as Nagel envisaged it, stipulates that the terms of two theories must be linked by what he called bridge laws, specifying the circumstances in which a term of the reducing theory can be substituted for a term of the theory being reduced. Imagine, for instance, that a theory T_1 contains the predicate F among its terms, that another theory T_2 contains the predicate G, and that T_1 is being reduced to T_2. A bridge law might state that whenever an object has the property F it also has the property G, and would then be used to deduce laws of T_1 containing the term F from laws of T_2 which contained the term G. This schema is not meant to do more than demonstrate in bare

---

[20] Perhaps the most influential of these critics are Thomas Kuhn, *The Structure of Scientific Revolutions* and P. K. Feyerabend. See Feyerabend, 'Explanation, Reduction and Empiricism' in H. Feigl and G. Maxwell, eds., *Scientific Explanation, Space & Time, Minnesota Studies in the Philosophy of Science* vol. III (Minneapolis, 1962) pp.28–97 and 'Reply to Criticism' in R. S. Cohen and M. W. Wartofsky, eds. *Boston Studies in the Philosophy of Science* vol. II (Boston, 1965) p.229.

[21] See, for example, M. Scriven, 'Explanations, Predictions and Laws' in F. Feigl and G. Maxwell, eds., *Scientific Explanation, Space & Time*, pp.170–230; R. Eberle, D. Kaplan and R. Montague, 'Hempel and Oppenheim on Explanation', *Philosophy of Science* 28 (1961) pp.418–28; W. Dray, *Laws and Explanation in History* (London, 1957).

[22] See, for example, T. Nickles, 'Two Concepts of Intertheoretic Reduction'; Marshall Spector, *Concepts of Reduction in Physical Science* (Philadelphia, 1978) pp.39–44.

outline how bridge laws are supposed to work, and neglects the various *ceteris paribus* clauses that usually surround connections such as that between F and G. Law-like connections between single predicates, licensing the substitution of F for G in all the laws of the reduced theory are an ideal that advocates of reduction might well strive for, but which they rarely achieve. In practice, as we shall see, bridge laws are more likely to relate predicates by links which can only operate in a comparatively narrow range of contexts.

It is important to notice that if reduction is to consist, in the traditional manner, in deducing the laws of one theory from those of another, then the bridge laws linking them must facilitate this. At best they will connect two type predicates, one from each of the theories concerned. A bridge law may assert, for example, that all the things held to possess the property F in T1 (or, to put it more technically, to be tokens of the type F) also have the property G in T2. Or they may link a disjunction of predicates from the reducing theory with a single predicate of the reduced one, yielding a statement of the form

$$(x)(P_1 x v Q_1 x v \ldots \supset P_2 x)$$

where $P_1, Q_1 \ldots$ are predicates of T1 and P_2 is a predicate of T2.[23] However, they may *not* connect a group of predicates of the reduced theory with a single predicate of the reducing theory, for while this would tell us that a predicate of T1 was associated sometimes with P_2, sometimes with Q_2 and so on, we would not then be able unambiguously to deduce the laws of T2 from those of T1. And the same goes for many-many connections between the two sets of predicates.

In practice it has often proved impossible to provide bridge laws satisfying these conditions. Among the obstacles impeding the reduction of Mendelian to molecular genetics, for example, is the difficulty of providing anything other than many-many connections between the gross phenotypic traits of Mendel's theory and the predicates of its molecular counterpart. 'Phenomena characterised by a single Mendelian predicate term can be produced by several different types of molecular mechanisms... Conversely, the same type of molecular mechanism can produce phenomena that

---

[23] Jerry A. Fodor, *The Language of Thought* (Hassocks, 1976) pp.2–26.

must be characterised by different Mendelian predicate terms.'[24]
The traditional conception of bridge laws may therefore sometimes
be criticised as inapplicable, and this is grave enough. But a still
more serious threat is posed by a different objection, which
questions the very idea of setting up law-like links between the
terms of distinct theories.

The root of this argument is the suggestion that it is a mistake
to try to take terms from a theory one by one, and find equivalents
for each of them. Such a strategy would be feasible if the theories
concerned were isomorphic in structure, so that the scope of a term
in one corresponded exactly to the scope of the equivalent term
in the other; but this state of affairs never obtains, because theories
do not in fact classify their subject-matters in precisely analogous
ways. Some philosophers then go on to claim that it is equally a
mistake to take the interrelated set of terms of which a theory is
composed and relate it in a law-like fashion to another set. The
reasons for this view, which are rather more complicated, rest on
the belief that every term of a theory gets its meaning from its
relations with all the others, so that each term means what it does
by virtue of its place in a network of laws and their implications.
As Feyerabend, a major exponent of this view, puts it, 'The
meaning of every theoretical term we use depends upon the
context in which it occurs. Words obtain their meanings by being
part of a theoretical system.'[25] This claim is sometimes thought
to pose a grave threat to an established view of scientific change.
For it is held to imply that theories are comparatively self-contained
units which cannot be translated into one another; it is not
possible to formulate connections between the terms of separate
theories that capture their meanings and are therefore applicable
in all contexts, because they simply do not match up in this way.
In Feyerabend's phrase, meanings are 'variant' between theories.[26]
If this view were correct, it would indeed have startling
implications, since it would suggest that it is actually impossible

[24] David Hull, *The Philosophy of Biological Science* (Englewood Cliffs, 1974) p.39.
See also K. Schaffner, 'The Peripherality of Reduction in the Development
of Molecular Biology' *Journal of the History of Biology* 7 (1964) pp.111–39, and
'The Watson–Crick Model and Reductionism', *British Journal of the Philosophy
of Science* 20 (1969) pp.325–48.
[25] P. K. Feyerabend, 'Problems of Empiricism' in R. G. Colodny, ed. *Beyond the
Edge of Certainty* (Englewood Cliffs, 1965) p.180.
[26] P. K. Feyerabend, 'Problems of Empiricism'.

to establish bridge laws between theories and hence reduce one theory to another. Rather than viewing the history of science as punctuated by reductions, in which theories are reduced from others of still greater power, we should see it as marked by a series of replacements – periods when scientists give up using a particular theory and turn instead to one which can do its work with more ease, economy or ideological purity.[27]

This thesis has been developed and studied in the context of the natural sciences. But its consequences for the social disciplines are equally dramatic. If there is no reduction at all, then there is obviously no question of reducing social theories to individual ones, and the issue will have to be reconsidered. Individualists would perhaps want to enquire whether theories can *replace* those about social wholes, and might try to formulate precise criteria for this relation. And holists might suggest reasons for concluding that theories about social wholes are not, after all, replaceable. But while this strategy has a lot to be said for it, some philosophers have argued that such a full retreat from reduction is by no means warranted on the basis of a Feyerabendian theory of meaning. Even if we accept the premise on which the replacement view is grounded, does it follow that bridge laws can never be established?

Those who argue that it does not, readily concede that the inter-definition of terms within theories stands in the way of establishing a complete set of bridge laws in the manner required by the traditional model of reduction. But they suggest that it is nevertheless sometimes possible to work out a set of practical equivalences between the terms of two theories which, although they do not allow one term to be substituted for another in all contexts, still guarantee this substitution in a significant range of cases.[28] Connections of this kind do not, of course, capture the full meanings of the terms concerned, and thus do not provide accurate translations. Nor do they state equivalences strong enough to establish that *whenever* a predicate F occurs in the laws of T_1 it can be substituted for the predicate G in the laws of T_2. Rather, they provide operational definitions of the terms of the reduced theory which are valid in a particular range of contexts.

---

[27] See, for example, Feyerabend's study of Galileo in *Against Method* (London, 1978) chs. VI–XIII.
[28] M. Hesse, *The Structure of Scientific Inference* ch. I.

In many cases the point of this exercise is to enable scientists to compare theories: if two rival hypotheses drawn from distinct theories are to be tested, it must be possible to formulate the experiment designed to judge between them and its results in terms that are acceptable to both sides in the dispute, a task facilitated by definitions of the sort just described.[29] Sometimes, however, such definitions may play the part of bridge laws, paving the way for reduction. For it may turn out that if you substitute the terms of T_1 for those of T_2 you will be able to deduce a fair proportion of the laws of T_2 and of the statements they imply, even though some laws will resist this process. The theories are thus seen as having what is sometimes called an area of intersection which opens up the possibility of testing one against the other, and offers a cut down version of reduction.

According to this view, the question of whether theories are reduced or replaced cannot be settled merely by appealing to contrasting theories of meaning. The post-empiricist belief that the meaning of a term is given by its place in a theory is not by itself enough to guarantee the conclusion that meanings are variant between theories. Rather, the degree to which they are variant in specific cases is a matter for investigation, and it is only through research that we can discover the extent, if any, of their incompatibility. At the same time, this approach offers a comparatively flexible account of the relations between theories, which can accommodate both reduction and replacement. At one extreme, it is conceivable that two theories might so match each other that one could be reduced to the other in the manner outlined by Nagel. In practice, however, it is more likely that they will intersect, in which case a limited reduction of the laws falling inside the area of intersection may be possible. Finally, the meanings of two theories may be variant, so that the relation between them can only be one of replacement.[30]

Theorists who are sympathetic to the view that terms get their meanings by virtue of their places in theories, yet who also believe that reduction can be achieved, are likely to favour such an

[29] *Ibid.*
[30] Hempel has suggested that Kemeny and Oppenheim's analysis of reduction, while not intended to describe this sort of case, does in fact fit it. See C. Hempel, 'Reduction: Ontological and Linguistic Facets' in S. Morgenbesser, P. Suppes, M. White eds. *Philosophy, Science and Method* (New York, 1969) p.142.

analysis. For by suggesting a modified form of the condition of connectability, designed to rule out those conflicting implications of theories which would stand in the way of deducing one set of laws from another, it retains the conception, if not the detail, of the traditional model. And by unshackling it from an outmoded distinction between theoretical and observable terms, and a too strongly referential theory of meaning, it appears to provide a means of updating our notion of reduction. This conciliatory path has many advantages. But it has nevertheless been criticised on the grounds that it is no more than a means of saving face, which conceals the fact that the underlying account of reduction has become enfeebled and scholastic. The basis of this complaint is the observation that the relation of reduction, as the conciliatory view conceives of it, only holds between those parts of theories that intersect. Since any laws or implications lying outside this region are left unconnected, it is only approximations of the theories concerned that are reduced. And the fruitfulness of studying the logical relations between idealised systems while neglecting their inconsistencies is clearly open to question.[31]

This doubt has been exacerbated by the practical difficulty of formulating bridge laws which allow reduction, even within the area of intersection of two theories. To establish one-one or many-one connections of the kind discussed earlier, it is often necessary to 'modify' or 'correct' the reduced theory considerably; and it then becomes natural to ask whether the modified version is the 'same' theory at all. In reply, it is usually claimed that the two forms must remain strongly analogous. For example, to return to the relation between Mendelian and molecular genetics,

In traditional Mendelian genetics, there exists a certain symmetry between dominance and recessiveness as well as a certain order of priority in series of epistatic genes. These two relations are combined in cases of dominant and recessive epistasis. One would expect these relations to be retained more or less in the corrected version of Mendelian genetics, which in turn might lead one to expect them to be reflected somewhat in the corresponding molecular mechanisms.[32]

Analogousness, however, is a matter of degree, and in cases where a theory has to be extensively reclassified in order for bridge laws

[31] P. K. Feyerabend, 'Explanation, Reduction and Empiricism'; K. Schaffner, 'Approaches to Reduction', *Philosophy of Science* 34 (1967) pp.137–47.
[32] David Hull, *The Philosophy of Biological Science* p.39.

to be formed, the question of whether it is really an existing theory that has been reduced, or something else, remains a troubling one.

How should theorists respond to this problem? The answer will partly depend on their beliefs about the significance and point of reduction, since the claim that it charts the formal relations between idealised theories may leave some rationales virtually untouched, while seriously undermining others. For example, the view that reduction aims to render theories obsolete and is thus a means to the simplification of scientific practice, is seriously damaged. A reduced theory will usually only be abandoned if *all* the explanations it yields are matched by those of the reducing theory; and this condition is only likely to be met if the reduction is complete. So if laws and generalisations lying outside the area of intersection of two theories are themselves used to explain certain sorts of phenomena, the theory may at least continue to be used in these contexts.

The attempt to defend reduction as a path to unified scientific practice is therefore jeopardised – or threatened – by this modified conception of the relation. But as we saw earlier on, it is more often valued as a contribution to our understanding than as a practical shortcut, and it remains to ask what impact recent criticisms of the traditional model have had on this justification. How does the incompleteness of reduction affect the suggestion that it elucidates the characters of both the reduced and reducing theories? For advocates of the hypothetico-deductive model, the matter was originally quite simple: the deduction of the reduced theory T_2 from the more powerful T_1 simultaneously explained it. And as long as we continue to assume that such deductions do indeed yield explanations, it seems that a partial reduction will explain those parts of T_2 that intersect with T_1, but not the rest. Like the account of reduction itself, the accompanying explanation will be modified, but essentially unchanged.

This phlegmatic approach has a number of advantages; but it neglects an important aspect of the problem which arises from the fact that partial reductions only succeed in deducing *some* of the laws and implications of T_2 from T_1. To assess whether the existence of this logical relation really amounts to a case of reduction, a judgment has to be made about the part played by the deduced laws and implications in the whole of the theory T_2. If they are regarded as constitutive of it, then reduction will be said to have been achieved, and may be justified on the grounds that it provides an explanation of the reduced theory. But if laws that are held to play an important explanatory role resist deduction, the attempt will be viewed as a failure. An assessment such as this is made in the light of a general interpretation of a theory which awards some of its laws greater importance than others on the basis of a variety of criteria. These may appeal to their explanatory role, their interrelations and so forth, or may be concerned, for example, with their impact on other theories. However, in either case, the question of whether an effort at reduction is successful is made to depend on more than a purely logical relation between the terms within the area of intersection of the theories concerned. As well as demonstrating the deducibility of the laws of a theory, the reduction must be shown to bear out an agreed interpretation.

Support for this analysis can to some extent be drawn from the evidence collected by philosophers of science about instances of reduction. Unfortunately, many of their claims are subject to dispute; but there are nevertheless enough studies to suggest that the rules for reduction are in practice neither fixed nor precise. It is claimed, for instance, that even in cases where it is not possible to deduce the implications of one theory from another, reduction is still held to be successful. Thus

An example of reducibility without deducibility is provided by 'tide theory' which no one would deny is reducible to mechanics — Newton's great unification accomplished this. Yet, specific tidal regularities (for particular places) simply cannot be deduced from basic mechanical laws (plus boundary conditions). The complexity involved is simply overwhelming. Another example is provided by that sub-domain of mechanics known as celestial mechanics. No one doubts that this is part of mechanics. Yet the systems involved are too complex to permit deducing detailed observed behaviour from basic mechanical laws. Certainly, before the advent of modern computers, there were many observed regularities involving planetary motions that could not be calculated on the basis of (deduced from) $F = ma$ plus the law of universal gravitation (plus boundary and initial conditions). Yet celestial phenomena of this sort were still (properly) considered to have been *reduced* to mechanics. After all, this was another part of Newton's great unification.[33]

Or, to take another kind of case, the condition of connectability is sometimes made more flexible than in the traditional account,

[33] M. Spector, *Concepts of Reduction in Physical Science* pp.40–41.

as when a set of bridge laws yield not the laws of a theory that is to be reduced, but consequences of them instead.[34]

Even if these particular examples prove to be contentious, there is nevertheless a balance of evidence in favour of the view that the relations between theories are various, and cannot be fitted into strictly-defined categories. Still more important for our argument, however, is the implication that the criteria for reduction are not simply logical, but include various qualitative considerations as well, a point which bears on the role of explanation in the reductive process. Traditionally, as we have seen, deduction was thought to guarantee explanation. But it now seems that broader explanatory criteria are actually used to keep the two conditions distinct, so that a relationship which is regarded as explanatory will be counted as a case of reduction even if the appropriate deductions have not been made. The attraction of this approach is clearly its ability to remedy something that its advocates regard as a serious flaw in the standard account – the fact that it is insensitive to the difference between sterile and fruitful examples of reduction. Logical criteria, they claim, are simply not adequate to capture the relation as it is experienced in the history of science, because they cannot reveal whether a reduction is, or is not, illuminating.[35] They therefore have to be supplemented by qualitative conditions, such as the stipulation that the corrected version of the reduced theory must indicate why the original theory was incorrect, or the qualification that the original theory must be explicable in a loose, informal sense by the reducing theory.[36]

The move to this more complex account of reduction is at once liberating in that it encourages philosophers to consider the whole gamut of relations between scientific theories, and at the same time confusing in so far as the conditions for reduction itself become more eclectic and interpretative. Especially vexing is the question of how wide a range of relations should be gathered into a single category, and several responses are common. Some writers, for example, wish to regard the replacement of one theory by another as a form of reduction, and thus make the category extremely

[34] *Ibid.*, p.39.
[35] Hilary Putnam, 'Reductionism and the Nature of Psychology', *Cognition* 2 (1972–3) pp.131–46. See also Andrew Lugg, 'Putnam on Reductionism', *Cognition* 3 (1973–4) pp.289–93.
[36] K. Schaffner, 'Approaches to Reduction'.

broad; others prefer to separate a group of reduction-like relations from replacement; and still others aim to maintain a strict definition of reduction, centred on the idea of deducibility. But this disagreement about how to divide up the terrain, which certainly admits of no conclusive solution, is in a sense secondary when compared with the underlying admission of diversity. The relations between theories cannot, it seems, be straitjacketed by rigorous definitions, and those that have been regarded by scientists as examples of reduction display no more than family resemblances. The pairs of theories concerned are shown to be logically connected along the lines we have discussed, and the relation between them is held to be explanatory. But neither of these conditions has clear priority, and they do not always go together.

This hard-won conclusion has emerged from meticulous studies of the relations between existing scientific theories, and repeated attempts to match up the evidence they have yielded with definitions of reduction. And since the resulting view is both more refined and less clearcut than its predecessors, it is at once a source of exhilaration and despondency.

On the encouraging side, we have an account of reduction shorn of any connection with the positivist doctrines discussed earlier in this chapter, which can be used to analyse and classify the connections between theories. On the less cheering side, however, reduction emerges as a multi-faceted relation, so that the task of assessing whether or not a theory has been reduced is both complex and highly interpretative. To judge the success of the reductionist approach to the problem of holism we must now see how holists and individualists accommodate to this account of the issue. Can individualists show that theories about social wholes have the requisite logical and qualitative relations with those about individuals? Or can holists show that they do not? These are the questions tackled in the next chapter.

II

Holism and reduction

The legacy of analytical philosophy, I have argued, has been to present the problem of holism as a problem about the reducibility of theories. Since the idea of reduction has primarily been derived from the study of theories about the natural world, philosophers of social science who put it to use implicitly assume a parallel between the social and the natural sciences; and the influence of the debates discussed in Chapter I has been so great that their findings continue to be widely used to make a case for or against the reducibility of social theories. The forms of reduction that individualists defend are those we have already considered.

The current conception of reduction is thus widely accepted as an appropriate means of settling the problem of holism; but it is nevertheless difficult to implement. The first and most obvious obstacle is the fact that the social sciences are not bodies of discrete theories. The idea implicit in many models of reduction – that the boundaries of theories are clearly marked out and the extent of their explanatory power agreed – is therefore often inapplicable; and while philosophers of social science may originally have set to work in the confident expectation that their disciplines would soon satisfy these requirements, their expectations are still unfulfilled. A second doubt concerns the method of proof employed by individualists to make their case. At first glance it seems that the most straightforward approach to their problem would be to treat it, in the manner of the natural sciences, in piecemeal fashion, and to examine the relations between specific theories to see if those about social wholes can be reduced. But this would not be enough. For although it would provide definitive answers in cases where reduction was successful, the dispute between holists and individualists demands a more ambitious remedy. Their disagreement is not simply about the reducibility of particular theories; rather, it concerns the question of whether all theories about social wholes are reducible in *principle*, even if they do not happen to have been reduced, and it can therefore only be resolved by a general argument. To prove the individualist's point it has to be shown that *all* social theories are reducible. And to substantiate the holist's claim it has to be demonstrated that at least *some* theories cannot be reduced. So the first task is to construct an argument of suitable generality. Thirdly, this approach to the problem of holism does of course reflect the belief that natural and social theories are sufficiently similar to display the same relations. And this in turn rests on the view that they share a common structure: if social theories, like natural ones, consist of sets of laws and their implications, then there seems no reason why it should not be possible to establish between them the logical and explanatory links that are definitive of reducibility. Theorists who defend or even consider this form of reducibility therefore take the line that social theories are – or ought to be – scientific, a view which is both hard to specify and hotly contested. Its ambiguity arises from the current debate about how the sciences themselves are to be characterised. And its contentiousness is due to the fact that many social scientists reject it outright, regarding their enterprises and explanations as quite unlike those of natural scientists. In their judgment the discussion in Chapter 1 is beside the point.[1] Some of these issues will be taken up later on. But rather than trying to approach the problem of holism by way of a discussion of the proper character of social science, I shall begin in a more modest spirit by asking what actually happens when holists and individualists attack or defend the reducibility of social theories. It soon becomes clear that both camps must face a common difficulty.

Until now, the problem of holism has been presented in rather crude terms as concerned with the relationship between theories about social wholes and theories about individuals: individualists claim that the former are always reducible to the latter, while holists deny that this is so. To consider the matter in any detail, however, we need a clearer conception of the difference between the two types of theory: what *are* theories about social wholes,

---

[1] This question trenches on the holism of form outlined in the Introduction. For a particularly apposite discussion see H. Dreyfus, 'Holism and Hermeneutics'; Charles Taylor, 'Understanding in Human Science', and Richard Rorty, 'A Reply to Dreyfus and Taylor', *The Review of Metaphysics* 34 (1980) pp. 3–55.

what *are* theories about individuals, and where is the line between them to be drawn? Unless these questions are answered, the individualist will be unable to take the first step in the process of reduction (that of showing that there are two groups of predicates that can be systematically related by bridge laws), and the holist will be unable to sustain any convincing counterargument. This issue is sometimes regarded as a tiresome preliminary to serious discussion, of no great importance. Yet it is absolutely central to the traditional debate, and has proved surprisingly resistant to any quick solution. Its recalcitrance is partly to be explained by the dearth of widely accepted social theories, so that the criteria for identifying theories of the two types cannot readily be derived from the social sciences themselves. But the problem has also been clouded by the existence of a number of conflicting opinions as to what is at stake in the dispute between holists and individualists, an aspect of the debate which emerges most clearly when one looks at the lines that theorists have attempted to draw.

How, then, are theories about social wholes to be separated off from those about individuals? Discussions of this question commonly begin by offering examples of sentences that are thought to fall squarely into the holist's or individualist's preserve: at one end of the spectrum are claims such as 'The CIA was strengthened by the President's reforms' or 'Britain pays a larger share of the EEC budget than France', which are unequivocally about social wholes of one sort or another; at the other end are those that describe individuals more or less independently of their social context, for example 'Leo is bald', or 'Her blood group is A positive.' Social theories are then defined as those containing laws and generalisations which attribute properties to social wholes, while individual ones attribute properties to individuals.

If this criterion were adequate, the difference between such theories would be easy to establish. Unfortunately, however, it is not sufficiently fine-drawn to provide a complete classification, and a large group of those sentences which are *about* individuals but nevertheless presuppose some social context fall between its two poles. When we say, for instance, that 'She was congratulated by the Prime Minister', or 'His wife is a heart surgeon', we attribute properties to individuals; but the properties themselves assume the existence of social wholes (governments, hospitals, etc.) and such sentences therefore seem to combine elements of both holism and individualism.[2] Since a large proportion of explanatory claims made by social scientists are of this type, the simple criterion we have just discussed does not serve, in practice, to isolate two groups of theories, and must be revised if the problem of holism is to be taken seriously.

With the aim of establishing a further criterion, some individualists have argued that, because sentences such as 'She was congratulated by the Prime Minister' are *about* individuals, they may consistently be incorporated in individualist theories, and only sentences that are actually *about* social wholes must be shown to be reducible.[3] This is obviously a prudent line to take, since the chance of producing a satisfactory theory made up of claims about individuals which do not presuppose some social content does seem, on the face of it, to be slight. But holists often object that individualists who opt for this solution are just letting holism in through the back door, since their explanations depend on the existence and influence of social wholes.[4] Both sides claim that they are entitled to use this contentious class of predicates in their theories, and they therefore cannot agree on where to draw the line between the two types.[5]

If serious argument is to get off the ground this disagreement must somehow be resolved, and proposals are duly offered by both sides. But they all run into difficulties. First, since any distinction between the two sorts of theories carries with it a view of what

[2] This triadic distinction is made by Robert Brown, *Rules and Laws in Sociology* p.138.

[3] J. W. N. Watkins, 'Historical Explanation in the Social Sciences', pp.169, 181; Alan Ryan, *The Philosophy of the Social Sciences* (London, 1970) p.177; Philip Pettit, *Judging Justice* (London, 1980) p.62.

[4] L. J. Goldstein, 'Two Theses of Methodological Individualism', in O'Neill ed. *Modes of Individualism and Collectivism* p.284; M. Mandelbaum, 'Societal Facts' in O'Neill ed. *Modes of Individualism and Collectivism* p.221. See also S. Lukes, 'Methodological Individualism Reconsidered' in *Essays in Social Theory* (London, 1977) pp.177–86.

[5] This discussion is complicated by a further debate as to whether S-predicates apply to anonymous or particular individuals. See K. Popper, *The Open Society and its Enemies* 2 vols. (London, 1946), vol. II p.226; J. W. N. Watkins, 'Methodological Individualism: A Reply', in O'Neill ed. *Modes of Individualism and Collectivism* pp.179–84; Alan Ryan, *The Philosophy of the Social Sciences* p.177; M. Bridgstock and M. Hyland, 'Reductionism: Comments on some Recent Work'; *The Philosophy of the Social Sciences* 4 (1974) pp.197–200; and 'The Nature of Individualist Explanation: A Further Analysis of Reduction', *The Philosophy of the Social Sciences* 8 (1978) pp.265–69; M. Martin, 'Reduction and Typical Individuals Again', *The Philosophy of the Social Sciences* 5 (1975) pp.307–8.

the project of reduction involves, and may prejudice the case for or against reducibility, none is to be accepted lightly. A suggestion made by one side may rest on assumptions not shared by the other. And to complicate matters still further, a number of the standard attempts to overcome the problem are designed to establish conclusions far stronger than anything the reductionist view requires. In one way or another, they aim to undermine the significance of the distinction between theories about individuals and theories about social wholes, and thus to cast doubt on the very idea that there are theories of two distinct types, one of which might be reducible to the other. The original question of how to distinguish them therefore tends to get swallowed up in this broader issue, and in the process is shelved rather than answered.

On the individualist side, arguments of this sort tend (like those discussed in Chapter 1) to bear the hallmarks of positivism, and to deal with the bone of contention between holism and individualism in what is by now a familiar fashion. As we saw, the central problem concerns the status of predicates which are attributed to individuals while also presupposing the existence of social wholes, and of these a large subset attribute mental properties about the social world to individuals. My thought that my union subscription is overdue or your desire to send your daughter to the local primary school each fall into this class, as do numerous other hopes, fears, beliefs, and other attitudes. Two reasons are commonly offered for thinking that these intensional properties can readily be incorporated in theories about individuals. First, when we attribute intensional properties about social wholes to individuals, we do not refer to the social wholes themselves, but rather to people's attitudes to them.[6] For example, the statement 'She believed the Home Office would give her a permit', is about an individual belief, not about the Home Office, and thus presents no difficulty. The second reason tries to meet a slightly more complicated objection:

[I]f we do not refer to institutions in characterising attitudes that have an institutional content, our opponent may yet claim that we have to make reference to institutions in explaining the formation of such attitudes. If an object is perceptually salient, in the sense that consistently with the perceptual clues and circumstances it is inevitable that the percipient identify it in some sense, then we may reasonably say that a

[6] D. H. Mellor, 'The Reduction of Society', *Philosophy* 57 (1982) p.66.

causal interaction between that object and the percipient accounts for the attitudes held in respect of it to which the perception gives rise. If I see water in the pan bubbling and come to believe that it is boiling, then it is not unreasonable to say that my belief is occasioned by a causal interaction, specifically the interaction characterising perception, between the water and me. The idea proposed by the institutionalist, is that a similar interaction between people and institutions must be postulated to explain the formation of certain attitudes which people hold in respect of the institutions and that we have to refer therefore to the institutions in accounting for that formation. However, the idea is surely unpersuasive. Institutions are not perceptually salient objects, for it is not inevitable that they will be identified under certain cues and circumstances: it will always depend on the percipients' having appropriate collateral beliefs, such as the belief that such-and-such treatment is typical of group behaviour, or that such-and-such reasoning is indicative of conformity to a practice. The perceptual interaction, therefore, that lies at the base of certain attitudes which agents form in respect of institutions is not interaction with the institutions themselves but with those items which they take as evidential tokens of institutions. Thus we are no more required to refer to institutions in explaining the origins of the attitudes which agents hold about them than we are in characterising the content of those attitudes.[7]

Before analysing this argument, let us ask what it would establish if it were right. It aims to show that, in order to explain the fact that individuals have all sorts of attitudes to social wholes such as institutions, we do not have to presuppose the *existence* of those social wholes, since we only need to take account of individual attitudes towards them. Such a view encounters two serious obstacles. One of these concerns the grounds on which the conclusion is defended – the dual claim that an object is only the cause of an attitude if the object is 'perceptually salient', allied to the further claim that institutions and other social wholes, unlike pans of bubbling water, lack this property. If we accept the stipulation that an object is perceptually salient when 'consistently with the perceptual cues and circumstances it is inevitable that the percipient identify it in some sense', then the conclusion about institutions is probably right; doubtless it is not *inevitable* that we should identify such social wholes in any particular circumstances. However, the contrast drawn between institutions and other

---

[7] Philip Pettit, *Judging Justice* p.63. See also G. Macdonald and P. Pettit, *Semantics and Social Science* (London, 1981) ch. III.

perceptually salient objects such as pans of bubbling water is a
highly contentious one, and many philosophers would deny
outright that objects of the latter sort are any more perceptually
salient than social wholes. This identification, they could claim,
depends on the percipients' 'having appropriate collateral beliefs',
and it is a mistake to suppose that we are simply bound to see them
for what they are. Implied in this criticism is the suggestion that
there may be no perceptually salient objects at all, a conclusion
which would do damage to the main thrust of the argument. For
it indicates that, if we wish to maintain a causal account of the
origin of at least some of our attitudes about the world, then
perceptual salience is an unsuitable criterion by which to judge
whether a particular intension is, or is not, caused. The central
claim of this individualist argument – that we can only give a
causal account of the origins of our attitudes about perceptually
salient objects – is thus open to considerable doubt, and would
need strenuous defence. And this weakness undermines the
plausibility of its conclusion that, in explaining people's attitudes
to social wholes, we need make no appeal to these wholes
themselves. For the holist claim that that is exactly what we *are*
doing is not disposed of, and the dispute with which we began
remains unresolved.

As well as analysing the steps by which an individualist might
try to dispel the worries of a holist opponent, it is enlightening
to pursue the second objection, which concerns their relation to
the main issue of reduction. An unspoken implication of this line
of reasoning is the belief that, at least as far as a large class of
intensional predicates is concerned, social theories do not have to
take account of institutions in the way that they must take account
of individuals. Individuals and their properties are the in-
dispensable stuff of enquiry, and are undoubtedly objects, out
there in the world. But institutions cannot claim this kind of
existence, and we need only appeal to them indirectly, as the
contents of individual attitudes. Such a view, like those discussed
in Chapter 1, overshoots the reductionist mark; for, instead of
claiming that reduction must be possible, it implies that there is
in a way nothing to reduce. In the intensional sphere, at least, all
we have to deal with are the intensional properties of individuals,
and our everyday appeals to institutions are no more than a short
cut – a quick, if inaccurate way of expressing truths about people's

attitudes.[8] So this is the sense in which the individualist claim to be able to use social predicates tends to get swept up in arguments stronger than anything needed to establish reducibility.

In a different form, the same fault afflicts the holist camp, and arguments designed to overcome the distinction between group and social predicates frequently depend on a set of assumptions which many individualists would reject. This can be seen, for example, in a highly influential article by Maurice Mandelbaum, in which he proposed a solution to the problem that has since become a standard part of the holist arsenal.[9]

Mandelbaum begins by distinguishing two classes of facts: societal facts, referring to 'the forms of organisation of a society'; and psychological facts, 'concerning the thoughts and actions of specific human beings'. Societal facts, he argues, cannot be reduced to psychological ones 'without remainder',[10] and to make this claim plausible he offers what is by now a famous example.

Suppose that I enter a bank, I then take a withdrawal slip and fill it out, I walk to a teller's window, I hand in my slip, he gives me money, I leave the bank and go on my way. Now suppose that you have been observing my actions and that you are accompanied by, let us say, a Trobriand Islander. If you wished to explain my behaviour, how would you proceed? You could explain the filling out of the withdrawal slip as a means which will lead to the teller's behaviour towards me, that is, as a means to his handing me some notes and coins; and you could explain the whole sequence of my actions as directed towards this particular end. You could then explain the significance which I attach to the possession of these notes and coins by following me and noting how the possession of them led other persons, such as assistants in shops, to give me goods because I gave them the notes and coins which the bank teller had handed to me. Such would be an explanation of my observed behaviour in terms of the behaviour of other specific individuals towards me. And it might at first appear as if an explanation couched in terms of these interpersonal forms of behaviour would be adequate to cover all of the aspects of the case.

However, it would also be necessary for you to inform the stranger who accompanies you that it does not suffice for a person to fill out such

---

[8] See Watkins, 'Ideal Types and Historical Explanation' in O'Neill ed. *Modes of Individualism and Collectivism.*

[9] Mandelbaum, '*Societal Facts*' in O'Neill ed. *Modes of Individualism and Collectivism*, pp.221–34. See also D. Ruben 'The Existence of Social Entities'.

[10] Mandelbaum, '*Societal Facts*', p.223.

a slip and hand it to just anyone he may happen to meet. It would also be only fair to inform him that before one can expect a bank teller to hand one money in exchange for a slip, one must have 'deposited' money. In short, one must explain at least the rudiments of a banking system to him. In doing so one is, of course, using concepts which refer to one aspect of the institutional organisation of our society, and this is precisely the point which I wish to make...In all cases of this sort, the actual behaviour of specific individuals towards one another is unintelligible unless one views their behaviour in terms of their status and roles, and the concepts of status and role are devoid of meaning unless one interprets them in terms of the organisation of the society to which the individuals belong.[11]

Mandelbaum next considers the predictable objection that, complicated though the process may be, there is no reason why statements about social institutions such as banks should not be analysed into statements about the attitudes and actions of individuals. But he argues that societal facts are not so easily expunged:

We have seen in the foregoing illustration that my own behaviour towards the bank teller is determined by his status. If the attempt is now made to interpret his status in terms of the recurrent patterns of behaviour which others exemplify in dealing with him, then *their* behaviour is left unexplained: each of them – no less than I – will only behave in this way because each recognises the teller of a bank to have a particular status. Similarly, it is impossible to resolve the bank teller's role into statements concerning his behaviour toward other individuals. If one wished to equate his societal role with his reactions towards those who behave in a particular way towards him, it would be unintelligible that he should hand us money when we present him with a withdrawal slip when he stands in his teller's cage, and yet that he would certainly refuse to do so if we were to present him with such a slip when we met him at a party. Bank tellers as well as depositors behave as they do because they assume certain societally defined roles under specific sets of circumstances. This being the case, it is impossible to escape the use of societal concepts in attempting to understand some aspects of individual behaviour: concepts involving the notions of status and role cannot themselves be reduced to a conjunction of statements in which these or other societal concepts do not appear.[12]

[11] *Ibid.*, p.224.
[12] *Ibid.*, p.225. This claim is also defended by E. Gellner, 'Explanation in History' in O'Neill ed. *Modes of Individualism and Collectivism*, p.262.

He therefore concludes that, in attempting to get rid of one reference to a societal fact we will find that others have been introduced, in a never-ending regress.

This attack on individualism is in a sense out of sympathy with the comparatively narrow question of whether one of two distinct types of theory can be reduced to the other. For although it employs the language of the standard debate, it actually suggests that the attempt to distinguish two sets of predicates is doomed to failure, and thereby attempts to obliterate the divide on which the individualist case depends. Like the individualist argument just considered, it is stronger than anything the reductionist strictly needs. And the gulf between it and the individualist approach to reduction is widened by the fact that Mandelbaum tacitly relies on a version of the holism of form discussed in the Introduction. Societal predicates cannot be expunged from explanations of social phenomena because they and individual predicates are interdefined, and it is therefore impossible to understand the meaning of one without the other. To put it another way, they are internally related.

In reply to this, individualists characteristically point out that Mandelbaum has not really *shown* that societal and individual facts are inseparable in the way he claims; he has merely stated it, and offered a single example designed to make his case plausible. Unimpressed by the theory of meaning on which his view depends, they then reassert their own claim that societal predicates can, after all, be reduced to individual ones.[13]

In this fashion, the debate between holists and individualists has frequently reached a stalemate. Individualist arguments are grounded on premises which holists do not accept, holist arguments make assumptions not shared by individualists, and the first requirement of reduction – the specifying of two types of theory each with its own predicates – remains unsatisfied. Yet the results of this discussion are not all negative, and Mandelbaum's attack on individualism, in particular, draws attention to an important feature of the individualist project which suggests a way out of this arid circle of argument.

The key to escape lies in the reminder, implicit in Mandelbaum's account, that what is at issue is the reduction of *theories* – of whole sets of interconnected laws and predicates. This point may seem

[13] Watkins 'Ideal Types', p.169n; Mellor, 'The Reduction of Society' p.66.

unduly elementary, but it is often forgotten by individualists, who base their claim that theories about social wholes are reducible on a few intuitive connections between specific predicates. There are, it is true, several ways of making such links. Suppose, for example, that a group, g, has members a, b, c,...n, and we attribute to it the predicates F, G, H...X; among the relations which can hold between the properties of g and those of a, b, c...n, are the following:

(1) Fg ⊃ Fa & Fb & Fc &...& Fn e.g. the group is in Marseilles if its members are in Marseilles.

(2) Fg ⊃ Ga & Gb & Gc &...& Gn e.g. the members of a board of trustees voting in favour of a motion constitutes the trust promising.

(3) Fg ⊃ Ga & Hb & Ic &...& Xn e.g. the group is influential in the locality by virtue of the fact that a is on the council, b is an estate agent, c has the borough surveyor in his pocket, etc.

However, while we can make these connections, it is not obvious what conclusions we should draw from them. They do give us good reason to believe that some sentences about groups can be 'translated' into sentences about individuals on the basis of our everyday language. For example, we habitually interpret 'the size of x' to mean 'the number of members of x' whether x is a flock of sheep or the population of Bangladesh, and there is perhaps no reason why this should not apply to social wholes in general. Because some of the phenomena dealt with by social theories are everyday ones, they rely heavily on descriptive terms taken over from ordinary language, which are only gradually modified to serve more specific purposes. But while ordinary language is sometimes an enlightening guide in this area it can also be misleading; and it is a mistake to infer the truth of individualism from the intuitive connections between sentences.

This is so for two reasons. First, there is more to reduction than connectability. And second, the possibility of establishing connections between propositions about social wholes and about individuals must be considered in a broader context than that of single pairs of sentences. The need for this is most pronounced in the case of propositions that do not occur in our everyday vocabulary; the predicate 'having a capitalist mode of production', for example, is defined in Marx's theory in terms of forces of production and production relations, which are in turn connected more or less directly to other states of affairs. It therefore cannot be 'translated' on its own. But the same is true of predicates applying to social wholes of which we have a greater intuitive grasp. The notion of something's being in one's interest, for example, which we attribute to individuals, is also applied to groups in situations where they stand to benefit from a course of action or events. Thus a general rise in the standard of living might be said to be in the interests of the working class, and on the basis of such examples we might conclude that something is in the interest of a group when it is in the interests of its members. Although this definition would have to be modified to fit cases where the group interest only corresponds to the interests of *some* members, there seems no reason why it should not cover a wide range of instances. However, when speaking of individuals one might want to include among their interests various considerations of which they are unconscious, and it is not immediately clear whether this conception of an interest can also be applied to groups.[14] Since we usually only attribute unconscious properties to creatures with minds it is often held to be inappropriate to talk about the unconscious interests of a group. Other theorists, however, argue that the notion of a group having real interests is perfectly intelligible and, indeed, vital to our understanding. At this point the analogy becomes vague, revealing one edge of the domain in which we can substitute propositions about individual interests for ones about group interests without begging a number of theoretical questions.

Another example of this phenomenon arises over the idea of decision-making, which we also attribute to groups on the basis of an analogy with individuals. In many circumstances we have

[14] The relation between the properties of individuals and those of groups is discussed by V. Held, 'Can a Random Collection of Individuals be Morally Responsible?' *Journal of Philosophy* 67 (1970) pp.471–81; P. French, 'Crowds and Corporations', *American Philosophical Quarterly* 19 (1982) pp.271–7, and 'The Corporation as a Moral Person', *American Philosophical Quarterly* 16 (1979) pp.207–15; D. Copp, 'Collective Actions and Secondary Actions', *American Philosophical Quarterly* 16 (1979) pp.177–86 and 'Hobbes on Artificial Persons and Collective Action', *Philosophical Review* 89 (1980) pp.579–606; A. Heller, 'Individual and Community', *Social Praxis* 1 (1973) pp.11–22; M. Olson, *The Logic of Collective Action* (Cambridge Mass., 1971); James Coleman 'Collective Decision and Collective Action' in *Philosophy, Politics and Society, IVth series*, ed. P. Laslett, W. G. Runciman, Q. Skinner (Oxford, 1972) p.208; *Power & the Structure of Society* (N.Y., 1974).

no qualms about replacing the sentence 'The group decided to x' with sentences about the decisions of individuals, and perhaps also information about the procedures by which decisions are arrived at. When we are thinking about individuals we connect the notion of decisions with various other concepts, including reasons and motives. Decisions are not made in isolation, but in the light of various considerations, and with certain ends in view; they form part of a network of individual behaviour. But when the concept is applied to groups, not all these connections hold. In particular, a group which has voted in favour of a course of action may be unable to give a reason for its decision, since each member may have a different reason for thinking it a good thing. Similarly, the group cannot always be said to have a motive, since those of the members may range from the virtuous to the criminal. So as well as a positive analogy between the decisions of individuals and groups, there is a negative analogy which prevents us from substituting one for the other in all contexts.

Theories about the behaviour of some classes of social wholes may begin, then, by taking predicates which are usually applied to individuals and extending them in a metaphorical fashion to groups. Some metaphors may turn out to be bad ones. But the criterion for a fruitful analogy is not that a claim should have exactly the same structure when made about social wholes as it originally had when made about individuals; it is meant, after all, to be enlightening. When a term is predicated of individuals it is part of a network of concepts. When it is applied to groups it will be part of another network which may be similar but not identical – for example, in the case of decision-making the link with reasons and motives is not retained. The terms and connections which the two networks share may fall inside the area of intersection of two of the theories; but the boundaries of this zone are a matter for empirical investigation.

This reminder of what is at stake in the dispute about reduction could in principle liberate it both from inconclusive demonstrations of the connections between particular predicates, and – more importantly – from fruitless attempts to draw a line between social and individual predicates. It thus might offer an escape from the dilemma which has so far dominated and hindered the discussion of reduction by suggesting a new way of distinguishing theories acceptable to holists from those favoured by individualists. This shift consists simply in a change of focus from the analysis of predicates to a concern with disciplines; instead of arguing about how to define two types of predicates, this approach concentrates on the broader question of whether the disciplines dealing primarily with groups can be reduced to those dealing primarily with individuals. For example, can sociology be reduced to individual psychology? And once again, individualists aim to provide a highly general argument to show that any theory which could properly be called sociological would indeed be reducible.

How, then, is this view defended? The first task, parallel to the thorny problem of separating out two types of predicates, is clearly to distinguish sociology from individual psychology. For example, one recent and representative account claims that

Sociology is about groups, and about people's social attributes; psychology is about their individual attributes. What their relation is depends therefore on which attributes are which, and that has not always been made clear...I gave being a capitalist and being the Pope as examples of social attributes, since they imply the existence of appropriately structured groups: no capitalist economy, no capitalists, no Church, no Pope. The same goes for all the examples in the literature, e.g. being a bank clerk. Merely *thinking* one is a bank clerk, or a capitalist, or the Pope, on the other hand, implies the existence of no such group: it is a purely psychological state.[15]

We have considered some of the reservations that a holist may already feel towards this definition; but putting those on one side, let us ask if it can be used to show that sociology is reducible to social psychology. How are we to demonstrate that 'all the sociological laws governing [the] properties and relations of groups [can] be acceptably approximated by adding law-like principles to the psychology, physiology and physics of people and other things beside groups'?[16]

The main plank of the individualist platform consists in the claim that the properties of social groups depend on what their individual members do. And the actions of individuals are in turn to be explained by their desires and beliefs, 'psychological states whose contents and strengths combine to cause specific activity'.[17]

The sociological properties of groups, and people's roles in them, depend therefore on psychological states of the people involved. Take

---

[15] Mellor, 'The Reduction of Society' p.66.
[16] *Ibid.*   [17] *Ibid.*, p.67.

an overt artefact group like Mandelbaum's bank. For someone to be a
bank clerk he must believe he is, as must the other bank staff and the
public, so that they act and react to him accordingly. The question is
whether these psychological facts suffice to make him a clerk. One reason
for denying it may be that a social mechanism is needed to confer this
role on him and to sustain him in it; a letter, or badge, for example...
   But what do such social mechanisms amount to? All they need to do
is produce the psychological states needed for social roles to be carried
out, and this they do by natural, not social means. The person to be
affected perceives a badge, a bank counter...He perceives these things
by no senses other than those available for perceiving inanimate things.
It is the shapes, colours, sounds, smells, tastes and feels of things that
make them known to us...A person must indeed learn to see things as
having the social significance they have; but that is just a matter of
becoming psychologically disposed to acquire the requisite beliefs and
other attitudes when he sees such significant things.
   I claim, therefore, that there is no more to the sociology of groups
than the psychological states which make people cooperate, more or less
consciously, in their social roles, and the natural mechanisms of action
and perception by which these roles are rightly or wrongly recognised
and carried out.[18]

   This argument reiterates a number of claims that we have
already discussed in connection with the distinction between
group and individual predicates, but they are here appealed to in
the name of a different conclusion – the reducibility of sociology
to individual psychology. In this respect, at least, this case for
individualism is superior to its predecessors, and is perhaps the
strongest available; so it is particularly important to ask whether,
in addition to being suggestive, it is successful. Does the claim
that there is a causal relation between the psychological properties
of individuals and the sociological attributes of groups really
suffice to show that sociology can be reduced?
   It is natural, I think, to register one immediate doubt: we do
not now possess a theory about the beliefs and desires of
individuals, conscious and unconscious, of sufficient strength to
provide a causal account of all sociological behaviour. It is true
that we make use of a number of fragments. But this defence of
reduction presupposes a unified theory that does not at the
moment exist, and its claim to be the proof of individualism is in
this respect hypothetical. Shrewd individualists will cast doubt on

                    [18] *Ibid.*, pp.68–9.

the significance of this fact by appealing to their own analysis: if the sociological properties of groups are just the effects of the psychological states of individuals, they will say, then there is no reason why we should not be able to build a complete psychological account, even though we do not have one at present. But this response draws attention to the stipulative character of the individualist argument; for, in advance of a fully-formed discipline, it lays down the requirement that sociology should be the study of those properties of groups which depend on individual action and are the causal outcome of individual beliefs and desires. If the doctrine of individualism, as it is here defended, is to apply to sociology in general, rather than merely to a selection of specific theories, then this criterion must be made definitive of the discipline.

There are, of course, powerful considerations in favour of this view. We habitually appeal to people's psychological states – in particular to their beliefs and desires – to explain their actions, and if the sociological properties of groups could be expressed as the causal outcome of actions then we would have a way of explaining them as well. Furthermore, we often *do* explain group properties in this fashion. However, the individualist is committed to defending the stronger claim that the procedure works for all sociological attributes, and this aspect of the argument is rather more murky. Certainly, sociologists of some persuasions countenance properties which fail to satisfy the individualist criterion; for instance the idea that groups can have collective interests which may not be reflected in the desires and aspirations of their members. Faced with such examples, individualists are inclined to discount them, on the grounds that they are figments of the imagination rather than genuine properties.[19] But this substitutes stipulation for argument, and it is difficult to see how the possibility that sociology could contain explanatory theories which deal with such attributes can be ruled out in advance. It is therefore not clear that this individualist argument demonstrates the reducibility of sociology as such, rather than of a subset of existing sociological theories. And even this weaker claim is, as I shall now suggest, open to doubt.

In discussing this case for individualism, we have so far taken

---

[19] J. W. N. Watkins, 'Methodological Individualism: A Reply' in O'Neill ed. *Modes of Individualism and Collectivism*, p.181.

for granted a particular conception of reduction; the view that all sociological laws governing the properties and relations of groups must be 'acceptably approximated by adding law-like principles to the psychology, physiology and physics of people and other things beside groups'.[20] But let us now stop to consider the chances of establishing bridge-laws between sociological and psychological predicates. As we saw in Chapter 1, reduction requires that two conditions should be met: the predicates of the relevant theories (or sets of theories) must be linked, either on a one-one, or a many-one basis; and the reducing science must explain phenomena that were previously elucidated by its reduced counterpart. That the first of these demands can prove an insuperable obstacle became clear from the example of genetics. For it was sometimes only possible to establish many-many connections between the terms of the classical and molecular theories, and even where more precise links were formulated, the degree of approximation involved was often so great as to cast doubt on the point of the enterprise.

If sociology is to be reducible to individual psychology, these pitfalls must be avoided. Yet, at an intuitive level, it seems quite likely that the connections between sociological and psychological properties will be of a many-many or a one-many form, and will thus be unsuited to the individualist's purposes. And even if the problem could be overcome by allowing some degree of approximation, we cannot say in general terms how much would be needed or how much would be acceptable, since it would depend on how it affected the explanatory force of the particular reduction concerned. These imponderables may well shake our confidence in the individualist claim, and also draw attention to the fact that it makes use of a rather strict criterion of reduction – one that places greater weight on the formal links between theories than on the explanatory relations between them.

The individualist case for the reducibility of theories about social wholes is thus far from proven, and there are strong grounds for believing that it cannot be completed. But in addition to these theoretical difficulties there is also a pragmatic one, which emerges as soon as we consider what would be involved in the sort of reduction that individualism requires. Whatever their other qualities, individualist explanations will clearly be enormously

[20] Mellor, 'The Reduction of Society' p.66.

cumbersome; consider, for example, the task of reducing a theory which contains group predicates such as those referring to the properties of institutions. In order to eliminate them, an individualist will presumably begin by charting the effects of individuals on individuals, and will then hope to derive composition rules to incorporate the effects of individuals on groups, groups on individuals and groups on groups. Such a scheme might be represented as a hierarchy of properties, by treating the characteristics of groups as properties of the properties of individuals (i.e. as second order properties) and then tracing the causal relations between the first and second orders. But even if comparatively simple claims about social wholes are replaced by such unwieldy statements about individuals, it is not obvious that the criteria for a successful reduction will be satisfied; for it remains to be seen whether the resulting theory can really be used to provide us with a rich understanding of the social world. Its sheer complexity might defeat the goal of explanation.

The failure of individualists to treat this objection seriously can be traced, I think, to their faith in the theory of the explanation of action on which their view depends, and I shall have more to say about this in the next chapter. Rather than avowing this allegiance, individualists usually prefer to sweep aside the charge of complexity as a merely practical obstacle, of no philosophical importance. But this judgment is surely questionable. If we are certain that individualist theories will provide us with better explanations than their holist counterparts, then certainly their awkwardness and size is just something we shall have to put up with. But if, in order for reduction to be successful, individualist theories must at least equal the explanatory power of holist ones, and if simplicity and applicability are allowed to be among the criteria for a good explanation, then it is by no means clear that individualism will surpass its rival. A realistic sense of what such reductions involve may lead us to question the point, as well as the feasibility, of the reductionist enterprise. If we can understand the social world in holist terms, why should we bother to reduce it to individualist ones?

When the problem of holism is equated with the issue of reducibility discussed in these two chapters, the major protagonists have unequal parts to play. The holist appears mainly as a foil for the starring role of the individualist, and the plot centres around the latter's desire to show conclusively that theories about social wholes are indeed reducible to theories about individuals. As we have seen, the argument for individualism must be strong enough to apply to social theories in general as well as to particular, extant examples of them, and the position is usually defended by appealing to a conception of reduction developed with the natural sciences in mind and then adapted to the social ones.

The results of this enterprise are, I have suggested, at best indecisive, and their inadequacy stems from their stipulative character. In the first place, current arguments for the reducibility of theories about social wholes rest on a view of the relations between two classes of predicates. But the claim that it is always possible to link social predicates (however these are construed) to individual ones, embodies an assumption about the nature of social theories which is itself open to dispute. While it may so happen that existing theories do not fall foul of it, it would be a tall order to demand that the social sciences should never transgress the criteria it imposes.

Perhaps the tantalising quality of the debate between holists and individualists is partly due to its hypothetical status. Because the relation of reducibility holds between particular theories or sets of theories, the claim that we cannot *now* reduce one theory to another does not imply that we will never be able to do so, and it is always open to the individualist to point this out. So defensive a strategy is obviously weak. But in the context of a tenaciously-pursued yet indecisive argument it is a valued last resort.

The upshot of the above argument is that, if any further progress is to be made towards understanding and resolving the problem of holism, the issue of reduction must somehow be bypassed. As we have seen, it is central to an established but fruitless debate which, I have sought to show, must now be put aside. To move forward, we shall have to delve deeper; and in the next chapter I shall attempt to do so by investigating the premises upon which the arguments mounted by each side are based. Once these are uncovered, we shall see that there is a far more fundamental incompatibility between the rival positions than current arguments have recognised.

Holism
and causal explanation

The arguments in defence of individualism discussed in the previous chapter are widely held to defeat holism utterly by demonstrating the reducibility of all theories about social wholes. But as we saw, this claim is asserted with more fervour than is justified, since the case for reduction is by no means watertight. In the first place, it is founded on a number of assumptions that many holists would reject. And equally important, it is made at a level of generality which has little connection with the work of social scientists. Because philosophical argument and social theory have floated so far apart, the debate about reduction is liable to seem trivial – an arcane preoccupation which has no counterpart in studies of particular social phenomena. If the problem of holism is to be returned to the world of social science, this gulf must be overcome. Theory and practice, as represented by philosophy and the various social disciplines, must be united, so that it is possible to investigate *existing* individualist and holist theories rather than hypothetical constructions.

In order to recast the problem, however, we need a deeper understanding of the divide between the two approaches, and must enquire why many individualists believe their view to be a decisive refutation of holism, while holists deny that it makes any headway at all. I have argued that the individualist case is far from being closed; but why do its exponents not see this for themselves? An indication that the issue is not quite as straightforward as the focus on reduction makes it seem can be gleaned from the high moral tone which pervades the discussion. Some individualists defend their view on the grounds that it not only provides simpler, more detailed and more perspicuous explanations than its rival, but that it is also *morally* superior to holism. For example, Karl Popper admonishes us that

All social phenomena, and especially the functioning of all social institutions, should always be understood as resulting from the decisions, actions, attitudes etc. of human individuals, and we should never be satisfied by explanations in terms of so-called collectives (states, nations, races, etc.).[1]

Here we are assailed by imperatives: we *must not* be satisfied by collective explanations, social phenomena *must* be understood in individualist terms. And although many individualists do not share this style and instead adopt the quasi-scientific voice of analytical philosophy, passages such as Popper's are nevertheless revealing. For they suggest that more is at stake in the dispute about holism than the comparatively technical notion of reducibility.

This impression is confirmed by other features of the debate between individualists and holists, including the fact that they continually talk past each other. A striking example of their dissociation is provided by the following exchange: on the one hand, Runciman takes it for granted that methodological individualism is 'now generally conceded to be almost trivially true',[2] while on the other Torrance asserts that 'In so far as methodological individualism is true it is trivial and irrelevant to sociology, while in so far as it is used to curb or dictate explanatory methods it is either incoherent or false'.[3] This mutual incomprehension could, of course, be accidental; but I will suggest that it expresses a division between the two positions which runs deeper than the dispute we have so far considered. Individualists and holists cannot agree about the reducibility of social theories because they approach the problem from different directions, and at the same time fail to recognise that this is so.[4] To understand what the issue is really about, we must look more carefully at the premises they bring to bear on the discussion of reduction; for this debate functions as a strait-jacket, stifling the very assumptions and aspirations which lie at the heart of the dispute.

[1] Karl Popper, *The Open Society and its Enemies*, vol. i, p.98.
[2] W. G. Runciman, *A Critique of Max Weber's Philosophy of the Social Sciences* (Cambridge, 1972) p.30.
[3] John Torrance, 'Methods and the Man', *Archives Européenes de Sociologie* 15 (1974). p.147.
[4] For further discussion of the moral implications of holism and individualism see K. Popper *The Open Society and its Enemies* vol. ii pp.69–70, 72–3; Isaiah Berlin, 'Historical Inevitability' in *Four Essays on Liberty* (Oxford, 1969) pp.43–68; J. W. N. Watkins, 'Methodological Individualism', p.172; S. Lukes, *Individualism* (Oxford, 1973).

The disparate perspectives of holism and individualism can best be appreciated by looking once again at individualism, and at the intuitions sustaining it. These amount, as we saw, to the belief that many social phenomena are to be explained as the outcome of actions performed by individuals or groups, and the view that groups can only do things if individuals do. A group action may not turn out exactly as the individuals involved intended; but in order for it to happen at all there must be individuals acting on the basis of various desires, beliefs and intentions. Thus, the actions of individuals are a condition of the actions of groups; and groups have no causal powers beyond those of individuals. As one exponent of individualism puts it with unusual explicitness,

The purpose of social institutions, where institutions may mean groups or practices, is to serve the interests of individuals…[S]uch institutions are intrinsically perfectible: they offer no resistance of themselves to being adapted to individual interests, although there may be other constraints on the adaptation possible. This reformist viewpoint represents groups and practices, in a metaphorical but not unwarranted characterisation, as playthings in the hands of people: instruments whereby individuals can better achieve their personal satisfaction. Not all institutions are supposed to have been the conscious project of individual ingenuity, but all are subject in principle to the ingenuity of the political planner.[5]

For our purposes it is important to consider what view of the individual underlies this claim. If we are to understand the philosophical assumptions that motivate individualism, we must ask what individuals need to be like for their causal powers to exhaust the causal powers of groups, and for the characteristics of groups to be explicable in terms of the characteristics of individuals.

First of all, there must be a strong asymmetry between individuals and groups. Within the boundaries of this mode of explaining social phenomena, individual agents are the root of explanation, a foundation for all the rest. And to fulfil this role they must be seen as independent of the society they help to constitute. If the traits of individuals were themselves determined by social groups of one sort or another, they would have to be construed as the playthings rather than the planners of institutions

---

[5] Philip Pettit, *Judging Justice* p.45.

and practices. So individualism must regard them as being in some
way free from the determining influence of society, and it is this
which makes the properties of individuals into a suitable stopping
point for explanations.

Some properties of individuals are nevertheless held to be more
significant than others. Although individualists allow that certain
types of individual property may be explained by appealing to the
properties of groups, they are committed to the view that other
individual properties *cannot* be explained in this fashion. And the
most important properties of which this is held to be true are those
which constitute our conception of individuals as autonomous
agents. This claim gives rise to an ontological dispute over the
nature of individuals, which underlies the issue of reducibility; for
holists and individualists disagree about how individuals are to be
characterised and what properties they possess. Are individuals
free agents who shape the social world according to their wills?
Or are they the products of society, constrained in their desires
and goals, as well as in their ability to realise them? Or are they
both?[6]

Stated in such crude terms, these alternatives are somewhat
bewildering; and yet their very crudeness serves to emphasise the
fundamental divide between holism and individualism. For if the
category of the individual is to play the central role allotted to it
by individualism, it must be the source of a number of social
characteristics which demand explanation. It must be possible to
trace these characteristics back to individual properties, and say
with confidence that these are what explain them. Treating
individuals as the end of the explanatory line in this way is
regarded by holists as a mistake. Rather than accepting this end
point, they want to push on and ask how individuals got the
properties – including their desires, intentions and so forth – that
are regarded as root causes by individualists. From their point of
view individualism gives up too soon, and thus fails to reveal a
whole dimension of the social world. But individualists, while they

[6] This dichotomy is a recurrent theme of social theory. For particularly
interesting discussions of it see Alan Dawe, 'The Two Sociologies', *British
Journal of Sociology* 21 (1970) p.207; Martin Hollis, *Models of Man* (Cambridge,
1977); Thomas Nagel, 'Subjective and Objective' in *Mortal Questions* (Cambridge, 1979) pp.196–213. A. Giddens, *Central Problems in Social Theory:
Action, Structure and Contradiction in Social Analysis* (London, 1979) ch. 1. For
a critical discussion of Dawe and Hollis, see Barry Smart, 'Foucault, Sociology
and the Problem of Human Agency', *Theory and Society* 11 (1982) pp.121–42.

can perfectly well understand this holist complaint, have not selected an arbitrary stopping-point. They think that, because of the kind of thing individual human beings are, they are bound to be the basis of social explanation. If it could be shown that, as some holists contend, those individual actions, decisions and choices which are appealed to in explanation, are themselves the causal outcomes of various larger states of social affairs, then individuals would not be of any special interest. They would be like cogs in a system of wheels, driven by social cogs and driving social cogs, but not contributing any new forces to the system. But individualism rests on the assumption that individuals are *not* like this: it is because they themselves contribute to the system of social life that they are so important in explaining it. And they are able to contribute in this way precisely because they are not determined by social factors, but possess the trait generally labelled autonomy.[7]

This difference between holists and individualists, hard as it is to formulate exactly, is a vital one: for it reveals the competing values which underlie the two approaches. Individualism, on this interpretation, is not adequately identified as the view that explanations must appeal to individual properties – the drives cited by behaviourists, for example, or the features of the unconscious invoked by psychoanalytic theories. Instead, individualism is motivated by a desire to defend the idea that individuals are autonomous agents, and thus tends to focus on a particular set of individual properties, including desires, choices, decisions and intentions. Later, in Parts II and III of this book, I will show how this analysis illuminates the debate between holists and individualists and the question of exactly how their positions are to be distinguished. First, however, I will argue that the ontological divide between the two views is reflected within the social sciences in a manner that reveals both the character of the dispute and its consequences.

The quest of holists and of individualists, each for a particular

---

[7] Of the recent works which aim to clarify our conception of autonomy, the following are particularly helpful. H. Frankfurt, 'Freedom of the Will and the Concept of a Person', *Journal of Philosophy* 63 (1971) pp.5–20; Donald Davidson, 'Freedom to Act' in T. Honderich, ed. *Essays on Freedom of Action* (London, 1973) pp.139–56; P. Strawson, 'Freedom and Resentment' in *Studies in the Philosophy of Thought and Action* (Oxford, 1968) pp.71–96; J. Rawls, 'Kantian Constructivism in Moral Theory', *The Journal of Philosophy* 78 (1981) pp.515–35.

type of explanation, marks the social sciences in two ways, one aggressive, one repressive. The latter symptom, common among individualists, manifests itself as a refusal to acknowledge the problem: while seeking to defend complex theoretical claims, individualists frequently take the intuitive truth of their own doctrine to be so overwhelmingly obvious that its opponents scarcely need to be taken seriously. Consider, for example, a recent attack on Braudel, which challenges his judgment that 'Charles V was an accident calculated, designed, prepared by Spain'[8] in the following terms:

> The very phraseology of the epigram deceives. 'Charles V', he begins, but he must mean the Empire not the person – 'was an accident calculated' and so forth 'by Spain' – yet there was no such thing in the late 15th century as a Spanish collective will. A handful... of rulers and their councillors were the match-makers, chief among them King Ferdinand of Aragon and Queen Isabella of Castille. We may safely rely on the dictum... 'the union of Spain and the Hapsburg lands was the last thing that Ferdinand and Isabella would have wished'. It needed a stillbirth and at least three unexpected deaths in the prime of life to bring about the empire of Charles V.[9]

Here, the claim that the empire of Charles V was calculated and designed by Spain is challenged on the grounds that 'there was no such thing in the late fifteenth century as a Spanish collective will'. Instead, there were various individuals – Ferdinand, Isabella and their councillors – and the fact that they did not *want* the unification of Spain and the Hapsburg lands is presented as decisive evidence against Braudel's view. But the latter can only be so quickly dismissed if the intentions of individual actors are the principal locus of explanation. And that is exactly what Braudel doubts, and what his opponents would have to demonstrate.

A similar case of *petitio principii* is to be found in Trevor Roper's presentation of the claim that good history emerges from imaginative counterfactual analyses of events and states of affairs. Attacking the crude Marxist theory which treats history as a law-governed and predictable process, Trevor Roper points out that the Marxist historians failed to predict the rise of fascism. And

---

[8] F. Braudel, *The Mediterranean and the Mediterranean World in the Age of Philip II*, 2 vols., trans. Sian Reynolds (London, 1972) p.519.
[9] Derek Beales, *History and Biography* (Cambridge, 1981) p.6.

how can anyone doubt, he goes on, that the course of the Second World War might in fact have been changed by a number of accidents.

How easily, in [1940, Hitler's] victory in the west might have been made final. I can think of at least four such hypothetical accidents any one of which might have had that effect. First, no one could rationally have assumed that at the precise moment of the fall of France there would be, in Britain, a statesman able to unite all parties, and the people, in the will and confidence to continue what could easily have been represented as a pointless struggle. The crisis does not always produce the man; moments of vital decision quickly pass; and in a period of confusion the power to act may be irrevocably lost. Equally, no one could have predicted that, at that historic moment, we would possess the vital secret intelligence – 'the Ultra Secret' – which, directly or indirectly, may have ensured the air victory over Britain... Thirdly, it was not reasonable to suppose, or even to hope, that General Franco, who after all had been placed in power by our enemies, would resist the temptation to which Mussolini had so easily yielded, and would refuse to rush to the aid of the apparent victor. Had Franco agreed to allow an assault on Gibraltar, that assault – as the experience of Crete and Singapore was to show – would probably have been successful. Then the Mediterranean sea would have been closed to Britain and a whole potential theatre of future war and victory would have been shut off. Finally, no one would have guessed that Mussolini would take it into his head to disrupt Hitler's plans for the invasion of Russia by a surprise invasion of Greece. Had any of these conditions been met, I believe that the whole history of the war might have been changed.[10]

Three out of four of these accidents fix on the properties of individual men as decisive variables directing the course of events: had Churchill been a less charismatic politician Britain might have given up her fight against Germany; had Franco permitted an assault on Gibraltar it would probably have fallen; and if Mussolini had not 'taken it into his head' to invade Greece, Hitler would have moved into Russia. And then everything would have been different. '...in 1940–1 a mere accident, and one which might easily have occurred, could...have reversed the outcome of the war and transformed the subsequent shape of the world'. The designation of such events as 'accidents' implies, as this statement

[10] Hugh Trevor Roper, 'History and Imagination' in H. Lloyd Jones, V. Pearl, B. Worden eds., *History and Imagination: Essays in Honour of H. R. Trevor Roper* (London, 1981) pp.360–1.

makes clear, that things could have been otherwise. Mussolini might have entertained another fancy, Churchill might have become too drunk to cope, and so on. But this assumption is what an opponent of a holist theory of history needs to defend. The claim that individuals are the proper locus of explanation because they could do otherwise, and the claim that their actions are indeed important independent variables which make a substantial difference to the course of events are precisely the claims that must be argued for, rather than merely stated. In short, the 'evidence' that Trevor Roper presents for his belief in 'historical free will' already presupposes it.[11]

Both these cases, while they are addressed to the distinct issues of whether history is accidental or planned, and whether it is accidental or law-governed, exemplify a widespread failure to engage with the problem of holism. For they beg the questions they ask by simply assuming the truth of individualism. This feature sharply distinguishes the repressive from the aggressive stance towards the dispute, which consists in holists and individualists giving incompatible answers to the questions they address, each set grounded on a prior commitment to their own approach. Like its counterpart, this symptom of an unresolved disagreement is extremely common in the social sciences, and crops up in all sorts of contexts. For example, E. P. Thompson[12] and Perry Anderson,[13] in a vivid exchange, debate the role of class-consciousness in the definition of the notion of social class. But the diverse views they defend can be traced, as I shall seek to show, to their holist or individualist assumptions.

For each writer, the problem at issue is the relationship between a social class and its members. Is it true, as Marx sometimes seems to say, that in order for a group of people to constitute a class they must be conscious of their shared identity, or can they form a class on the basis of other criteria? Thompson, the individualist, takes the view that consciousness *is* a condition of class identity:

Classes arise because men and women, in determinate productive relations, identify their antagonistic interests and come to struggle, to

[11] For more reflective discussions of this problem, see James Joll, 'Politicians and the Freedom to Choose', in A. Ryan ed. *The Idea of Freedom* (Oxford, 1979) pp.99–114, and John Dunn, 'Understanding Revolutions', *Ethics* 92 (1982) pp.299–315.
[12] E. P. Thompson, *The Poverty of Theory and Other Essays* (London, 1978).
[13] Perry Anderson, *Arguments within English Marxism* (London, 1980).

think and to value in class ways. Thus the process of class formation is a process of self-making, although under conditions which are 'given'.[14]

To identify classes you have to go back to the intentional properties of individuals – to the judgments, desires and aspirations which are essential to explaining what they then *do* in the class struggle. Anderson, by contrast, rejects this view:

Classes have frequently existed whose members did not 'identify their antagonistic interests' in any process of common clarification or struggle. Indeed, it is probable that for most of historical time this was the rule rather than the exception...Did Athenian slaves in ancient Greece, or class-ridden villagers in medieval India, or Meiji workers in modern Japan 'come to struggle, to think in class ways'? There is every evidence to the contrary. Yet did they thereby cease to compose classes? Thompson's error is to make an abusive generalisation from the English experience he has studied himself...the result is a definition of class that is far too voluntarist and subjectivist.[15]

This dispute demonstrates particularly plainly that the underlying divide between holism and individualism is a crucial feature of contemporary social science. At a superficial level it produces incompatible definitions so that, despite their having the word in common, Thompson and Anderson use 'class' in different ways. It might of course be claimed that this is all that has to be sorted out: just tidy up the definitions, and the problem will be resolved. But, perhaps unfortunately, the causes and consequences of the dilemma go deeper than this suggestion implies. Thompson's and Anderson's choices of their respective definitions are clearly the fruit of a more fundamental attachment – to the underlying assumptions of individualism in Thompson's case and to holism in Anderson's – and as the tone of their exchange reveals, they will not lightly give these up. To point out the difference between their conceptions of class is, in consequence, simply to state a more fundamental problem. Moreover, their use of their disparate conceptions does not just lead them to give contradictory answers to common questions such as 'Were Athenian slaves a class or not?' Both can ask this, both can answer it, and both can see why the other gives the opposite reply. Once this ground-clearing is done, however, it becomes evident that Thompson and Anderson,

[14] E. P. Thompson, *The Poverty of Theory* pp.298–9.
[15] Perry Anderson, *Arguments within English Marxism* p.40.

like individualists and holists in general, are in fact approaching their subject-matter by asking quite different questions. When Thompson asks about the emergence of classes he enquires into the choices and intentions of individuals, which are for him a crucial kind of evidence, and sees the process of class formation as one of self-making. When Anderson broaches the same task he investigates modes of production and the relationships they confer on individuals. For him it is at best idiosyncratic to speak, in Thompson's celebrated phrase, of the 'making' of a class. Instead, 'it is, it must be, the dominant *mode of production* that confers fundamental unity on a social formation, allocating their objective positions to the classes within it, and distributing the agents within each class'.[16]

Andersons's insistence that the notion of social class must be defined in structural terms can be traced to an over-riding commitment to holism. He rejects the criteria favoured by Thompson not, of course, out of mere dogmatism, but rather because he believes that the self-consciousness of a class is not a crucial factor in explaining its birth and development. And why not? Either because its causal impact is outweighed by structural considerations (a possibility that will be discussed in Chapter VI), or because it is itself to be explained as the effect of social wholes and their properties.

The rift that divides Thompson and Anderson commonly afflicts practising historians and social scientists in their attempts to explain particular phenomena. As a result, it is quite common to find competing explanations of a single set of events, each presupposing the truth of just those premises – whether holist or individualist – which themselves require to be established. Consider, for example, the long-standing dispute among economic historians about the causes of the industrial revolution in England. This question has given rise to a whole spectrum of views, whose exponents are united by two traits: their desire to explain why an industrial revolution occurred in Britain and not in other comparable nations, and their adherence to the Millean method of difference. They agree that to isolate the causes of the revolution one must search for factors which were present in Britain and absent in, say, France or Belgium. However, when they begin to suggest what these factors might be, it emerges that they have

[16] *Ibid.*, p.55.

markedly different conceptions of what will provide an adequate explanation. There are, first of all, historians who believe that the crucial variable must lie with the psychological characteristics of a comparatively small group of entrepreneurs, who instituted changes in the technology and organisation of industry: British entrepreneurs are held to have displayed a peculiar wit and resource in expanding and transforming production and distribution – a wit which is not itself subjected to scrutiny.[17] However, this form of individualism is more often tempered by the acknowledgement that social factors at least exert some formative influence on character, with the result that the individualist element of explanation is somewhat muted. This middle position is well expressed by Mathias.

The entrepreneurs...were not the long lost cause of the industrial revolution. They sprang from economic opportunity as much as they created it. They depended everywhere upon a necessary creative environment. They join the circle of other factors in economic growth as part cause and part effect, a dependent attribute and a creative part of industrial progress. But they are important. Latent resources can lie unused until 'men of wit and resource' organise them for a market they have promoted. Once formed attitudes, often consolidated within social groups, exert an inertia of their own, like institutions, for good or ill.[18]

Individualism of this variety strives to put individuals in their social context, but nevertheless gives them the last laugh. Ultimately, it is up to individuals to make something of their situation, and their motives and capacities therefore play a central part in explanation – they have, so to speak, the casting vote. Contrasted with it are explanations which explicitly subordinate individuals to social factors of one sort or another. For example, in asking why the French did not innovate like the British, one historian turns straight to economic factors.

...Technological progress is closely bound up with economic phenomena, and the explanation we are looking for must be first and foremost

---

[17] T. S. Ashton, *The Industrial Revolution* (London, 1948) p.161; See also E. Hagen, 'On the Theory of Social Change' in T. Burns and S. Saul, eds., *Social Theory and Economic Change* (London, 1967).

[18] Peter Mathias, *The First Industrial Nation* (London, 1969) p.151. See also C. Wilson, 'The Entrepreneur in the Industrial Revolution in Britain', *History* (1957) p.111.

an economic one. The contention is that the French, unlike the British, did not innovate because they were not made to do so by the strong pressure of economic forces.[19]

As before, these manifestos propound a variety of views about how to answer a single question. Each picks out a different type of factor and claims that it is the key to a causal understanding of the Industrial Revolution; and in doing so, each relies on an undefended account of the assumptions that need to be embodied in satisfactory explanations.

The difficulty, then, with all the cases I have discussed – and with a large number of other disputes of a like kind – is that each side argues past the other by assuming the truth of what has to be proved. To gain a clearer understanding of the differences between such schools of thought, and thus to see what the opposition between holism and individualism consists in, it is therefore essential to try to do something that the protagonists in such debates themselves seem unwilling to attempt; to give a more precise account of the conflicting conceptions of individuals and their capacities that underlie these disagreements.

It might appear, from the arguments and prejudices just considered, that the nature of the commitment dividing holists from individualists has already emerged: holists, it seems, are in effect determinists, and it is this feature of their theories that individualists are anxious to reject. But before accepting these equations it is important to ask both whether they are well-founded, and whether they are a means to a better understanding of the relatively specific problem of holism. I shall suggest that, although they capture some superficial similarities between the two issues, they are ultimately misleading.

One reason why the shift in emphasis to the broader question of determinism is less helpful than it at first appears is that 'the problem of determinism' itself lacks a clear formulation,[20] and the difficulty of saying exactly what it consists in is reflected in attempts to relate it to holism. Various links have been proposed

[19] F. Crouzet, 'England and France in the Eighteenth Century: a Comparative Analysis of Two Economic Growths' in R. M. Hartwell ed., *The Causes of the Industrial Revolution in England* (London, 1967) p.161.

[20] For an interesting formulation of this difficulty, see T. Nagel, 'Subjective and Objective' p.198.

and discussed, but they are on the whole more revealing of the
disparity between the two problems than of their convergence.
This is apparent, for example, in the view that identifies determinism as the thesis that every event, together with some other
event, is an instance of a natural law, so that there is a law-like
connection holding between each event under some description
or other, and another event.[21] As it stands, this claim will be of
no explanatory interest if the relevant descriptions of events are
trivial in the light of our projects and concerns, and a persuasive
conception of determinism must therefore include some method
of selecting from among the multifarious possible descriptions of
events those that are considered to be significant. Different
standards of significance will naturally yield different theories –
sets of laws relating significant descriptions. And the proof of
determinism would presumably consist in showing that an all-
embracing theory of the kind envisaged can be constructed, a
theory incorporating every event under some significant
description.[22] However, it is not clear that arguments for or
against this possibility will cast light on the differences between
holists and individualists concerned with social explanation. For
as Wiggins points out,

Economic events, say, or commercial events, could be part of a larger
deterministic system without themselves (or as such) comprising a
self-contained deterministic system. And it would not follow from the
fact that any system they helped to make up was deterministic that the
laws in virtue of which it was deterministic would be *laws of economics*
or *laws of sociology*. Even if every state or event which is of sociological
or economic interest is implied by some physical state or event X in virtue
of some physical laws L, it does not follow that either X or L can be
expressed in purely economic or sociological terms.[23]

Since this formulation of determinism cannot help us, perhaps
we shall do better to concentrate, as a number of theorists have
done, on a different one: the claim that every event has a cause.
Holists, it is sometimes suggested, subscribe to this view, while
individualists reject it in favour of the belief that individuals are
capable of free, or autonomous, action. At the outset, this

[21] David Wiggins, 'Towards a Reasonable Libertarianism' in Honderich ed.,
Essays on Freedom of Action, p.36.
[22] See Wiggins's account of saturated descriptions, 'Towards a Reasonable
Libertarianism' p.39.
[23] *Ibid.*, pp.40–1.

dichotomy looks comparatively promising, but once again the equation of determinism with holism on the one hand, and of non-determinism with individualism on the other, gives rise to difficulties. First, if holism and individualism are to be distinct, causation and autonomy must be mutually exclusive categories: if the autonomous character of action is to stand in the way of the truth of determinism, actions cannot at the same time be caused. However, we are then faced with the question of what we are to understand by autonomy. If autonomous actions are said to be *un*caused (and hence undetermined) they are left completely mysterious, and the prospects for individualism as a set of explanatory theories look very weak indeed.[24] But if they are caused, their existence cannot, after all, be used to falsify the thesis of determinism.

Discussions of the exact meaning of autonomy are absent in the debate between holists and individualists. Almost all individualists are willing to concede that actions have some causal antecedents, since they allow that people are shaped and constrained by environmental factors which form their personalities and affect what they do. They take it for granted, for instance, that

Inheritance and environment direct a man's actions. They suggest to him both the means and the ends. He lives not *in abstracto*; he lives as a son of his family (and of wider social groups)... He does not himself create his ideas and his standards of value; he borrows them from other people.[25]

But this does not get in the way of the conclusion that

If we scrutinise the meaning of the various actions performed by individuals we must necessarily learn everything about the actions of collective wholes. For a social collective has no existence and reality outside of the individual members' actions.[26]

If their commitment to the central explanatory role of the individual is not to be undermined by concessions such as these, individualists must believe that environmental factors cannot carry all the explanatory weight. They undoubtedly contribute. But there must be a point beyond which they cannot go – some remaining 'self' to which social scientists appeal.

[24] For this point see Thomas Nagel, 'Subjective and Objective' p.198.
[25] L. Von Mises, *Human Action: A Treatise on Economics* (London, 1949) p.46.
[26] *Ibid.*, p.42.

As this self is debated and discussed, the individualist sometimes seems to be demanding that a *ceteris paribus* clause should be included in all explanations of social phenomena – a murmured oath of loyalty to the freedom of the will along the lines of ' ... and the individuals involved could have done otherwise'. Such a clause would not bring the dispute between holists and individualists any nearer to a solution, however, since it begs the very question at issue. Nor would the dispute be of any great interest, because the explanatory role allotted to individual autonomy is so minimal. In order to sustain a more robust disagreement, individualist theorists must contend that human autonomy makes a substantial difference to the explanation of action, and stands in the way of the determinist account supposedly favoured by holists.

The assimilation of individualism to this version of anti-determinism presents the individualist with an intractable dilemma. If actions are uncaused then it is not clear how they are to be explained, while, if they are caused, they are not autonomous. And the assimilation of holism to determinism leaves holists in an equally unpalatable position. For the hypothesis that every event has a cause does not make the distinction between the causal powers of social wholes and those of individuals which is central to their view. Thus neither side is any further forward, and each is adventitiously yoked to the vicissitudes of a complex metaphysical issue.

To gain a richer understanding of the problem of holism we must therefore distinguish it from the problem of determinism. Rather than treating holism and individualism as exemplifying two qualitatively different types of explanation – the causal and non-causal, lawlike and non-lawlike – they are more accurately conceived as concerned with the relative priority of two kinds of causal factor in the explanation of social phenomena. As we have seen, individualists are anxious to explain social states of affairs as the outcome of individual actions and attitudes which cannot themselves be explained as the outcome of social states of affairs. This by no means commits them to the view that actions and attitudes are uncaused, merely to the more limited view that they are not caused by the properties of social wholes. Holists, by contrast, wish to explain individual intensions and desires as the outcome of these wholes, thereby awarding explanatory priority to a range of social factors the identity of which varies from theory to theory. Each party to this dispute is happy to allow that there are two kinds of causal factor, individual and social, which play a part in explanation. It is their status and relationship which is the subject of disagreement.

Once the problem of holism is construed in this fashion, it can readily be unshackled from the various questions surrounding the idea of determinism; and at the same time, there becomes available a more perspicuous account of the notion of autonomy on which the individualist case depends. For, instead of being tantamount to the mysterious suggestion that actions are uncaused, the claim that they are autonomous can be interpreted as a summing up of the individualist view that they must be explained, at least in part, by appealing to the intentional properties of individuals. Like individualism itself, it becomes a claim about the *kind* of causal factors that will provide us with an understanding of the social world.

As soon as the question is posed in this fashion, however, it begins to look as though some form of individualist answer is bound to be preferred. For there is no doubt that our prevailing intuitions about ourselves as agents, and a number of associated philosophical arguments about the concepts of choice, action and responsibility, have tended to make the case of individualism seem not merely strong, but so compelling that we have no option but to accept it.

The persuasiveness of this judgment is widely attested; but before we can gauge its force, we must consider the grounds for standing by this form of individualism. A particularly incisive and economical analysis of the reasons for doing so has been provided by Strawson, and his argument, though by no means the only one of its kind, presents an exceptionally strong case.[27] Strawson begins his discussion with an account of what he calls the 'reactive attitudes' which we display to others whenever we treat them as responsible moral agents, capable of forming and acting on intentions. Relationships of this kind, including most of those between normal adults, give a place to emotions such as resentment, gratitude, forgiveness or disappointment which are only appropriate when we believe that someone's behaviour towards us was conscious and intentional. It is fitting to feel resentful, for example, when we have been wantonly injured; but for an injury to be

[27] P. F. Strawson, 'Freedom and Resentment'.

wanton it must satisfy these conditions. Reactive attitudes of this sort are contrasted with so-called 'objective' ones, which we adopt towards agents who are not regarded as morally responsible: thus we often try not to resent injuries done to us by small children or the mad, because we recognise that, in some sense, they do not know what they are doing.

The familiarity of this divide at least seems to show that we do not *treat* all behaviour as determined, and thus that a distinction between autonomous and non-autonomous individuals is part of our everyday conception of the world. These are the intuitions that give holist and individualist explanations their initial plausibility. However, Strawson also draws a stronger conclusion from it – the conclusion that, since a theory of the determination of action is true now if it is true at all, such a theory would have to be compatible with our distinction between behaviour towards which reactive attitudes are appropriate, and behaviour demanding an objective response. Admittedly, he says, some behaviour is regarded as externally caused in as far as the *real* explanation is not the intentional one. But not all behaviour can be explicable in this fashion, because if it were, we should be unable to distinguish the neurotic from the normal. Strawson's claim is that abnormal behaviour, as its name implies, is defined negatively as behaviour towards which our normal responses are not fitting. Thus it is only by reference to a standard of normality that we can identify and respond to actions such as those of children and the insane.

Strawson is surely right to emphasise the distinction we currently make between what we regard as non-intentional and intentional behaviour, and to remind us that we react to these categories in very different ways. For while an objective attitude carries with it a certain distance, and a recognition that what we think of as natural responses such as gratitude or resentment are out of place, reactive attitudes confirm our beliefs about the expectations people have of one another in society. If we now ask how we could discover that all action is to be explained in non-intentional terms, and at the same time take the point that it could not be non-intentional in the way that mad or childish behaviour is, it seems that we should have to come to see all action quite differently. For we should have to be able to redescribe both the actions we currently regard as rational, and those we think of as requiring a reactive response, so as to overcome the contrast between them. Short of actually achieving this, it is hard to imagine how we would then perceive social relations, and what sort of responses would seem appropriate to the actions of others. But it does *not* follow, as Strawson asserts that it does, that we should have to take an objective attitude to all behaviour just like the attitude we now take to behaviour we call abnormal. If the sense in which all behaviour was non-autonomous turned out to be the same as the sense in which abnormal behaviour is now understood to be so, then the same attitude to it would be appropriate. But as we have just seen, Strawson gives us reason to think that it *cannot* be explicable in just this sense, and he is therefore mistaken in concluding that a holist theory would involve us in responding objectively to all actions.

Thus it is not clear what it would be like to regard all actions as requiring non-intentional explanation, and this makes it much harder for the individualist to argue that, whatever it would be like, it is out of the question. However, Strawson goes on to suggest that the transformation in our attitudes which would be needed if we ever came to believe that all our actions had this character is beyond our capacities.

A sustained objectivity of interpersonal attitude, and the human isolation which that would entail, does not seem to be something of which human beings would be capable, even if some general truth were a theoretical ground for it.[28]

This claim about human nature is then followed by the assertion that we could never gain adequate evidence for a holist theory, and so could never give up our view of individuals as basically autonomous actors:

This commitment [to ordinary interpersonal attitudes] is part of the general framework of human life, not something that can come up for review as particular cases can come up for review within this general framework.[29]

This last claim extends the bounds of Strawson's project. For as well as suggesting that if we were to give up the view that most actions are autonomous we should have to give up a great deal else as well, it asserts that this transformation of our attitudes is

---

[28] *Ibid.*, p.82.   [29] *Ibid.*, p.84.

actually beyond us. We cannot imagine what it would be like. And it is inconceivable that we could ever achieve it. However, neither of these claims is self-evident as it stands, and a quizzical holist will want to question their force. In the first place, the limits of the imagination are shifting sands, and it is not obvious that anything which at present lies outside them is forever beyond our grasp. It is certainly true that, when offered an explanation that conflicts with our beliefs, we can reject the explanation on the ground that, since our beliefs are true, it must be false. But we can also modify our beliefs to accommodate it. By way of reply, Strawson can of course fall back on his belief that this is not true of our commitment to reactive attitudes because it is part of 'the general framework of human life', which *cannot* be given up. Again, though, a holist may question the assertion that there *are* such privileged features of our understanding, and may suggest that even our most fundamental attitudes are not immune from revision.

The type of argument exemplified by Strawson's claim undoubtedly has a strong intuitive appeal, and versions of this approach have, ever since Kant, been popular as a means of seeking to set limits to the use of causal explanations in accounting for human affairs. But so far as the problem of holism is concerned, attempts to formulate such *a priori* defences of individualism are unsatisfactory in two ways. Although they aim to carve out an inviolable space for individualist explanation, the boundaries of this area remain unspecified; *some* human behaviour, it is allowed, requires a holistic approach; but when does individualism give way to holism and *vice versa*? Strawson himself relies entirely on an intuitive sense of the line between them, but we can see from the history of the social sciences that such intuitions change with time and place. The work of Freud, for example, has so entered our habits of thought that we now label 'objective' various forms of behaviour which would formerly have been regarded as reactive.

The second difficulty arises from the fact that this defence of individualism rests on an idea of a 'general framework of human life' which is itself open to doubt, and would be challenged by a number of holists.[30] Like the differences discussed earlier in this chapter, the split between holists and individualists over what is

[30] See Part II.

to be accepted as given runs extremely deep, and cannot readily be resolved on its own. Since the two views belong to opposed epistemological theories, neither side is likely to be easily convinced by the other's arguments.

This latter conflict is a grave one. It gives rise, moreover, to an even graver reservation about the efficacy of arguments which rely on our intuitions about agency. As we have seen, Strawson's analysis gains its plausibility from the fact that it is based on an appeal to our everyday view of ourselves, which is offered as an *a priori* reason for adopting an individualist approach. This defence of individualism is then taken to define the limits of holism as a viable form of explanation. But such an argument implicitly rules out an important alternative; for it discounts the idea that the attempt to give an *a priori* defence of individualism may be mistaken. If this excluded option is allowed back into the debate, and the claim that our existing intuitions should not be given the last word is seriously considered, the authority of the case for individualism is immediately questioned. Instead of being taken for granted as a set of explanatory standards which will bolster and enhance our understanding of the social world, individualism may appear to offer only a narrow and distorting lens through which to inspect it.

The source of this subversive suggestion is the view, already mentioned in the Introduction, that social theorists who adhere too closely to a single set of explanatory canons are liable to put themselves at a disadvantage. Entering the kitchen with an explicit recipe for explanation, individualists are liable to reject any hypotheses which fail to conform to their requirements, on the grounds that they do not provide an adequate account of the phenomena with which they are concerned. This strategy may, however, be a mistake. For it neglects the possibility that, by studying the conjectures and procedures of social scientists, we might arrive at a richer and enlarged conception of social explanation. Once we see that the relationship between a set of explanatory principles and the more specific analyses offered by social scientists must be a reciprocal one we are able to benefit from the fact that, just as social scientific practice is moulded by existing views of explanation, so those views can be refined and altered by the impact of practice.

Once this idea is accepted in principle, it remains to ask at what stage a grasp of the mutual dependence between social theory and social science might be capable of helping us with the problem of holism. My answer is: at the precise stage we have now reached in the argument. As I have sought to show in the present chapter, the philosophical grounds on which individualism is defended, though compelling at first sight, are in fact open to doubt. For there is no good reason to subscribe to the widely-held intuition that explanations have to conform to individualist tenets. But if this is so, not only is the case against holism once more put in doubt, the case for supposing that it can ever be established in such an *a priori* fashion is threatened at the same time. If we are to make any further progress, then, we must now abandon the assumption that the practice of the social sciences must conform to our existing philosophical intuitions, and instead consider seriously the possibility that we might be able to develop a better theory of social explanation by way of examining the successful practice of the social sciences.

This is accordingly the method which, in Part II, I propose to adopt. I shall single out those writers whom I take to be the most significant among contemporary anti-individualist social scientists; I shall examine in some detail the nature of the assumptions embedded in their practice; and I shall seek to assess the coherence of the social explanations those assumptions lead them to produce. I shall approach their work, in short, in the light of the pragmatist belief that a study of the problems they pose and the solutions they offer may provide us not merely with a new perspective on the scope of holistic explanations, but also with the best means, in the end, of assessing their strength.

PART II

Practice: holism in social explanation

IV

Absolute holism
and its framework: Althusser

Holism, as we have seen, is defined as the view that social
phenomena are to be explained by appealing primarily to the
properties of social wholes, since the latter are the causal factors
which shape the characteristics of individual members of society.
This analysis sums up a view which is embraced with varying
degrees of enthusiasm. At their most confident, holists expect to
supersede the need for *any* individualist explanations, and thus
undertake to provide powerful and wide-ranging social theories.
In their more tentative moods, by contrast, they simply claim a
place for their approach, leaving its scope a matter for debate. But
in both cases, holists are united by a commitment to the explanatory
primacy of the properties of social wholes that guides and informs
their research.

In this section I shall explore the strongest of the range of holist
positions – the view that there is no place at all for individualist
explanations of the social world. By investigating the ways in
which it has been used to explain particular phenomena, I shall
aim to provide a more detailed account of absolute holism, as I
shall call it, and of the mode of explanation it embodies. This task
is made all the more necessary by the fact that opponents of
absolute holism often find it strongly counter-intuitive, not to say
absurd; although they can grasp it at a very general level, they have
difficulty in imagining either how it could be developed, or what
would make it plausible. To overcome this barrier, I suggest, one
must look at the approach in action; only then will it be possible
to see what it has achieved, and to assess what it might achieve
if taken on its own terms. In this chapter I therefore discuss what
I take to be the strongest case for absolute holism in contemporary
social science, the case expounded by Louis Althusser.

Before embarking on this project, however, two preliminaries
must be dealt with – a qualification and a question. The qualifica-

tion concerns the fact that holism cannot be studied on its own. It is always a characteristic of theories which have many other features, and since it refers to a general *kind* of explanation rather than to explanations which make use of any particular set of categories, it is compatible with social theories of many types. They may be categorised as Marxist, like Althusser's, as structuralist (in some senses of the term), as functionalist, and so on. Any attempt to grapple with a holist theory will therefore have to separate its holist character from its other features, and especially where a theory is weak, it will be important to see whether the deficiency is the result of its being holist, or is due to something else. For example, Althusser's belief that new theories are the fruit of epistemological breaks or 'ruptures' with what went before is fraught with difficulty. But it has comparatively little to do with his holistic claim that individuals are merely the 'supports' or 'bearers' of social practices. By contrast, his account of the epistemological status of Marxism is intimately connected with this, since the holistic relation between practices and individuals is intended to destroy the idea of the individual as the locus of knowledge, and therefore calls for major epistemological reforms. The closeness of these links is obviously a matter of degree, since there will always be some connection between the various aspects of a theory; but a concern with the general problem of holism will inevitably constrain us to see a theory in a particular perspective, and to focus sharply on certain characteristics at the expense of others.

Since this would be true whatever theory we were to select, it remains to ask what makes the works of Althusser and Poulantzas especially well-suited to our purposes. At first glance, the association of holism with their strongly materialist brand of Marxism might seem to prejudice the discussion: the very distinctiveness of its explanatory categories might seem to distract attention from the matter in hand. In fact, however, the unqualified character of Althusser's claims are among their advantages. He defends a position which denies that the properties of individuals are ever explanatory, and which therefore falls squarely into the domain of holism as this was outlined in Chapter III. And since absolute holism can be used, in Althusser's view, to explain a wide range of phenomena – to explain how societies are organised and maintained and how they change – his theory provides an opportunity to assess both the character of his approach and its scope. But as well as having this comparatively obvious advantage, Althusser's awareness of the radical implications of his claims makes them all the more interesting. With unusual explicitness, he states the grounds and consequences of his approach, and in addition to grappling with the task of offering holist explanations, he addresses its epistemological corollaries. His account is therefore by far the most ambitious and the most insightful of its kind, and is of singular value as an instantiation of, and a means to assess, absolute holism.

Partly for this reason his work has been, and remains, enormously influential among social theorists, who are variously attracted and repelled by it. Some are content to praise or vilify Althusser while never engaging deeply with his views, and many of the debates surrounding his work are conducted at this superficial level. Others, however, have made serious and much-needed efforts to explore the consequences of his theory. For Althusser's claims are by no means easy to understand, and one reason for this is the fact that they are all exceedingly general, so that it is often unclear how they are to be used for the vital task of explaining particular states of affairs. If the theory is to exemplify and test holism, the project of discovering whether, or how, it can be applied, is obviously extremely urgent, and among Althusser's followers, the person who has made the greatest strides in this direction is undoubtedly Nicos Poulantzas. Poulantzas appeals to Althusser's theory to resolve the long-standing problem of how to characterise the capitalist state – and in doing so casts light on its power and its limitations.

To investigate this kind of holism, then, I shall begin by laying out the most relevant portions of Althusser's theory. Next, I shall discuss some difficulties which it either generates or leaves unsolved. In Chapter v I shall move on to ask whether the work done by Poulantzas suggests a means of overcoming these problems, and finally I shall consider how successful the theory is as a tool for furnishing explanations of the social world.

To appreciate Althusser's work one must first of all understand why so much of it takes the form of an exposition and defence of Marx's writings. Both the book entitled *For Marx*,[1] and

---

[1] *For Marx*, trans. Ben Brewster (London, 1965). Hereafter abbreviated to FM.

Althusser's essay in *Reading Capital*[2] are elaborate interpretations of Marx's views, and this fact is not explained by the simple observation that Althusser himself is a Marxist, anxious to give an account of the theory of history to which he is politically committed. Numerous theorists approach their work armed with interpretations or modified versions of Marxism, and to stick so firmly to elucidating Marx's own texts might seem a rather scholastic project, in the pejorative sense of that phrase. But Althusser puts it to dramatic use. For he claims that, despite all the attention it has received, Marx's doctrine has been radically misunderstood and underestimated. And he aims, by careful exegesis, to reveal it to a community of intellectuals who 'have not yet realised, or have refused to recognise it'.[3] His task is therefore two-fold: he must identify the ways in which Marx has been misread, and provide an account of the work which will lay bare its awesome originality. As far as Althusser is concerned, the resulting theory is not only Marx's but also true.

In order to do this Althusser arms himself with a method for dealing with his material which he borrows from hermeneutics. This is the idea of a 'symptomatic reading' of the relevant texts, a reading designed to master the superficial characteristics of Marx's criticisms of Hegelian idealism and classical economy, and of his own views of political economy and society, and at the same time yield a deeper understanding of his whole project. By paying careful attention to what Marx fails to say (his 'silences') as well as to what he makes explicit, Althusser hopes to recover two things: the questions Marx was trying to answer, and the general theoretical assumptions underlying his replies.[4] The justification for wishing to unmask these hidden features of Marx's work is obvious, since an awareness of the questions he failed to ask would enable us to understand more clearly what he was trying to do, and what he regarded as a satisfactory answer to his dilemmas. But the enterprise itself is interpretatively taxing, since Althusser claims that Marx never consciously formulated his own theoretical position. He knew, needless to say, that his analysis of the role of the economy in social life was revolutionary, but never realised

---

[2] Louis Althusser and Etienne Balibar *Reading Capital*, trans. Ben Brewster (London, 1970). Hereafter abbreviated to RC.

[3] Althusser, 'Philosophy as a Revolutionary Weapon', *New Left Review* 64 (1970) p.3

[4] RC, pp.25–6.

the extent to which it was based on a radical philosophy. 'Contrary to certain appearances, or at any rate to my expectations, Marx's methodological reflections in *Capital* do not give us a developed concept, nor even an *explicit* concept of the *object of Marxist philosophy*. They always provide a means to recognise, identify and focus on it, and finally to think it, but often at the end of a long investigation, and only after piercing the enigma contained in certain expressions.'[5] Althusser therefore employs this method to recover from Marx's work something its author never clearly expressed.

The difficulties of this task are compounded by a natural unwillingness to admit any independent criteria for judging a particular reading, since Althusser's aim is to interpret Marx in his own terms, rather than to impose on him any independent (and ideological) standards. The point is not to approach the texts with preconceived ideas about matters such as what constitutes an argument, what provides evidence for a claim, or when we can be said to know something. It is rather to see how Marx handles these problems, and what views he holds about them. Althusser therefore defends a circular method of enquiry. Marx's work cannot be understood in any terms other than the ones he himself developed; but these are not spelled out, and are only indirectly expressed in his work. Therefore it is necessary to read his work in order to master the philosophical principles which enable one to understand it. Althusser puts the point like this:

The theory which permits us to understand Marx – to distinguish science from ideology, to understand the difference in their historical relations, the discontinuity made by the epistemological break in the process of history, the theory which enables us to distinguish words and concepts, the existence or non-existence of a concept in a certain word, to discern the existence of a concept in the function of a word in theoretical discourse, to define the nature of a concept by its function in the problematic and by its place in the theory – is itself Marxist philosophy.[6]

A symptomatic reading is therefore a condition of a symptomatic reading, and an interpretation of Marx can only be judged in terms of its internal coherence.

One outcome of this exercise is the claim that Marx's philosophical views are to be found in *Capital* rather than in his earlier

[5] RC, p.74.   [6] FM, p.39.

writing, and Althusser argues that this work, in particular, has been misunderstood. It is usually interpreted as a critique of classical economy, combined with an alternative suggestion about how economic phenomena can be understood. Like classical theory, Marx's proposal is said to yield various empirical predictions, so that time and experience will enable us to test both positions. Although this is by any standards a grotesquely over-simplified account of hundreds of pages, it brings out the attitude which Althusser contests – the idea that Marx's theory of political economy is just an *alternative* to the classical one, in that crucial experiments can be devised to adjudicate between them. When we compare such a view with that of Althusser, we can see why he feels so strongly that the *scope* of Marx's theory has not been recognised. For he believes that Marx constructed an altogether new *kind of* theory, of a novelty and importance comparable to the discoveries of Newton or Galileo, and with a structure quite unlike those of its predecessors. 'Marx founded a new science: the *science of the history* of social formations, or the science of history. The foundation of the science of history by Marx is the most important theoretical event of contemporary history.'[7] Very briefly, Althusser first of all argues that this theory is built upon new concepts (such as the forces and relations of production) which have no counterpart in the classical theory of political economy. Furthermore, even where Marx appears to adopt existing terms (such as surplus value, which seems to combine Ricardo's notions of rent, profit and interest), their relations with other concepts in the theory, and hence their meanings, are changed. But as well as having a novel structure, the theory has an explanatory power quite unlike that of classical economics: for while the latter attempted to explain economic systems as a response to individual needs, Marx accounted for a much wider range of social phenomena in terms of the part they played in a totality. *Capital* therefore provides us not just with a view of the economy, but with a way of analysing the structure and development of a whole society. Underlying this 'discovery' Althusser claims to find a revolutionary epistemology which centres around the abolition of the distinction between subject and object, and makes Marx's theory incompatible with those of his predecessors.

7 Althusser, *Politics and History*, trans. Ben Brewster (London, 1972) p.166.

The last part of this reading is the most profound, and is of great interest both as an exegesis of Marx, and as a general philosophical position. In order to grasp it in detail, however, one must be familiar with the model of social structure which Althusser attributes to Marx.

In so far as one can single out a starting-point in Althusser's exposition, it is Marx's critique of *homo oeconomicus*. Classical economy is said to have assumed that all men are alike in sharing certain needs which must be satisfied if they are to survive, but which can be met in a variety of ways. This 'anthropological' approach was the root of notions of production, exchange and consumption, which were thought to apply universally and were used to explain the economic arrangements of existing societies. Marx offered two well-known criticisms of this view. First, he argued that it is highly artificial to construe all consumption as a response to needs; while this approach may seem illuminating when it is applied to the consumption of individuals, it cannot plausibly be extended to productive consumption, which has to be treated as 'the consumption which satisfies the needs of production', if the theory is to be sustained.[8] Secondly, he rejects the very assumption of classical theory that economic phenomena can ultimately be explained as the result of universal needs. Instead, Marx argues that the needs of individuals are a function of their social environment. It is true that everyone needs to eat to stay alive, but biological requirements of this sort are too 'basic' to have much explanatory power; we do not so much wish to understand why societies produce food as why they produce different kinds of food in different ways. And we cannot explain more complex needs by appealing to a concept of a universal individual such as *homo oeconomicus*.

While Marx rejects needs as the units in terms of which economic phenomena should be analysed, he could in principle simply replace them by some other property of individuals, and found a theory on this trait instead. But he does not adopt this alternative, and his criticism of needs is in fact part of a much more fundamental attack on classical economics. For the attempt to explain social phenomena in terms of needs presupposes that they are 'given' concepts which we can apply relatively easily, and use as a basis for enquiry. In our attempt to understand a group of

[8] RC, p.165.

complex phenomena we pick on some 'simple' starting-point such as a need, and proceed to treat it as though it were completely transparent. Marx is deeply opposed to the idea that a theory has a 'starting-point', and in particular to the claim that social phenomena can be explained as the result of universal properties of individuals, and Althusser sums up his scepticism with an epigrammatic flourish: the classical idea that man makes his own history must be countered with the question 'How is the man who makes history made?'[9] 'The individual producer, or the individual as the elementary subject of production, which eighteenth century mythology imagined to be at the origin of society's economic development...only appeared, even as an "appearance" in developed capitalist society, that is, in the society which had developed the social character of production to the highest degree.'[10]

By way of solving this problem Marx suggests that individuals are formed by their social context, by the whole collection of physical conditions, conventions, rules and beliefs which make up their experience. When Althusser develops this claim, attempting to minimise the value of individual traits as a basis for generalisation, he suggests that not only each society, but each *class*, 'makes its own individuals'[11] because its social environment differs substantially from that of other classes. (Thus a German worker in an advanced capitalist society has more in common with a British worker than with a German industrialist.) However, the force of the overall argument is only marginally affected by this modification. For Marx is trying to develop a theory which will apply universally, and the fact (if it is a fact) that individuals who live in different societies do not share constant properties is enough to disqualify them from being the rock on which social explanations are founded. As well as implying this criticism of classical economy, Marx's attitude suggests a new approach to the construction of a social theory. Any attempt to pick out one concept, such as that of an individual, and theorise about it, will always be vulnerable to the challenge, 'But how is that concept to be explained?' In one sense this is simply to point out that we can always demand to have an explanation explained. However, Marx

[9] Althusser, *Réponse à John Lewis* (Paris, 1973) p. 18. Hereafter abbreviated to RJL.   [10] FM, p.196.   [11] RJL, p.18.

might argue that because the character of societies is what it is, the demand is not superfluous in the case of social theory, but is a particularly pertinent one. There are some natural phenomena which we generally explain in terms of the workings of their parts, and if asked for a more detailed account, we discuss the relations between smaller and smaller parts. And although there may be a limit after which no more can be said, we do not describe a full circle and return to the proposition from which we began. Classical economy took this view of the explanation of economic phenomena; it explained complex economic systems in terms of their parts, and reached its limit at the level of individual needs. But Marx opposes this approach, on the grounds that human needs do not spring out of nothing, and suggests instead that a theory must be constructed which has no 'starting-point'. For if the relations between the individual and society are as close as he believes, we must take them into account; instead of grounding explanations upon one part we must theorise about the whole to which all the parts belong.

Nevertheless, a social theorist has to start somewhere. Rather than analysing society in terms of one kind of component, Althusser claims that Marx breaks it up into related units called, in Althusserean parlance, 'practices'. The advantage they have over individuals is that, although each practice only contains a part of the complex phenomenon which is society, each one is a 'whole' in the sense that it consists of a variety of different *kinds* of parts, all of which are interrelated. For example, economic practice contains raw materials, individual men, tools, etc., all united in a more or less institutionalised process. Instead of thinking of society as made up of simple parts, we must think of it as a collection of wholes which together make up one 'complex whole'.[12] However, if Marx's theory is to be universally applicable, it must be built around practices which are common to all societies. Althusser, in his later work, identifies three of these – economic practice, ideological practice, politico-legal practice – and gives an account of them which draws heavily on Marx's discussion of the process of production.

This analysis is, as we shall see, extremely important to his overall position. He argues that although there is no such thing as production 'in general' since, in Marx's words, 'When we talk

[12] FM, p.199.

of production we always mean production of individuals living in society,[13] nevertheless all forms of production have some things in common. They all use a particular means of production to transform raw materials into a product, whether of a material, political, ideological or theoretical character. Thus a practice is distinguished by a particular mode of production, adapted to its own kind of product. The mode of economic production prevalent in a society may be very different from the mode of ideological production, but they can still be said to share certain ingredients.

There can be no scientific conception of practice without a precise distinction between the distinct practices...We can assert the *primacy of practice* theoretically by showing that all the levels of social existence are the sites of distinct practices: economic practice, political practice, ideological practice, technical practice...We think the content of these different practices by thinking their peculiar structure, which, in all these cases, is the structure of a production; by thinking what distinguishes between these different structures; i.e., the different nature of the objects to which they apply, of the means of production and of the relations within which they produce.[14]

The claim that the complex whole of society should be seen as consisting of practices is an attempt to get away from the idea that a social theory can be grounded upon a concept which is 'simple' and 'given'. However, in order to maintain the advantage gained by thinking in terms of practices rather than individuals, it is important to guard against the danger of tacitly converting a practice into a 'starting-point'. For just as the properties of individuals are dependent on their social context, the set of social relations which constitutes a practice does not exist in isolation. Althusser portrays Marx as extremely sensitive to this possibility, and appeals to his awareness of it in a further argument about the position of economic practice in the complex whole. This attempts to refute a common interpretation of Marx's work and can help us to understand Althusser's reading in greater detail.

The argument attacks the position that Marxism is crudely materialist in regarding theoretical, political and ideological practices as determined by the economic base. Apart from the inherent implausibility of this claim, Althusser argues that if Marx

[13] K. Marx, *Introduction to the Grundrisse*, trans. M. Nicolaus (Harmondsworth, 1973) p.85.   [14] RC, p.58.

were to defend it he would be vulnerable to the very criticism
which he made of classical economy. For just as Marx, when faced
with the problem 'How does man make his history?' replied with
another question, 'How is the man who makes history made?',
so the proposal that the economic organisation of a society
determines its superstructure should prompt us to ask how the
base itself is determined. The parallel between these questions is,
in Althusser's view, matched by Marx's answers. Just as Marx
criticised the suggestion that we could found a theory on universal
human needs, he now rejects the idea that we can introduce an
independently defined notion of economic practice and use it to
explain other aspects of society. Instead we have to recognise that
all practices are dependent on each other and are interdefined. As
an example of this interconnection Althusser points out that
among the relations of production of capitalist societies are the
buying and selling of labour power by capitalists and workers.
These relations, which are part of economic practice, can only exist
in the context of a legal system which establishes individual agents
as buyers and sellers. And this arrangement, in turn, may have to
be maintained by political or ideological means. We can therefore
see that certain aspects of economic practice depend upon the
so-called superstructure, as well as the other way round, and
Althusser concludes that it is a serious error to neglect this aspect
of Marx's theory. 'The whole superstructure of the society
considered is thus implicit and present in a specific way in the
relations of production, i.e. in the fixed structure of the distribution
of the means of production and economic functions between
determinate categories of production agents.'[15]

This argument against a crude materialist interpretation of Marx
is presented as an application of the claim that social phenomena
cannot be explained by appealing to a 'given' concept. The same
claim is then made the basis of an attack on the classical notion
of what an economy *is*. By taking certain needs to be universal,
classical theory not only committed itself to a particular approach,
but also defined its subject-matter. For anything to do with the
satisfaction of these needs was counted as an economic phenomenon, and thus not only the explanatory structure of the theory,
but also its content, was taken to be constant. Althusser's

[15] RC, pp.177–8.

discussion implies that the same will be true of all theories which have independently defined starting-points, and the identification of this link between the terms of a theory and its subject-matter is an example of the way in which Althusser tries to uncover the assumptions underlying the classical and Marxist views – what he calls their 'problematics'.[16] He aims to show that concepts which appear to be independent are actually *inter*dependent, so that one cannot abandon one and leave the others intact. However, it remains to ask how Marx, with no starting-point to appeal to, defines the economic sphere. How does the analysis of society into related practices affect our conception of what is included in economic practice? In considering this question Althusser indicates the limits of Marx's approach. He presumably wants to say that the idea that there can be a general definition of the economic sphere is a residue of the classical claim that it is defined in terms of some universal trait such as human needs. For Marx's view that there is no such thing as production in general has the consequence that there is no *economic* production in general, but only the modes of production used by particular societies at particular times. And since economic practice is defined by a mode of production, the character of a given economic practice will be determined by the whole of which it is an element, and may be quite unlike its counterparts in other societies. Nevertheless it will have a counterpart. For according to Althusser, Marx takes the notions of certain practices as primitive, and assumes that they will be present in all societies. Their characters will vary enormously, but since all communities must produce in order to survive, there will always be something identifiable as economic practice.

Although Althusser does not say so, there is thus a puzzle at the heart of his interpretation of Marx. On the one hand, Marx is applauded for having escaped both from a theory which founds its explanations on a conception of individual needs, and from the very idea of a 'starting-point'. But on the other hand he is said to have posited a trio of practices, which fulfil the same function in his own account. Practices are, to be sure, a very different place to start from individuals. But this part of Althusser's more ambitious claim for Marx as the founder of an altogether new kind of theory is not upheld.

Instead of what we might call a vertical analysis of society – one

---

[16] FM, p.70.

which builds upon a single kind of term – Althusser attributes a horizontal analysis to Marx. We can best understand the nature of societies and the ways in which they change by investigating the relations between practices. It is on these that we must concentrate in order to gain a knowledge of society as a 'complex structured whole'.[17]

We have seen that, according to Althusser's reading, Marx is committed to arguing that practices are mutually dependent, and some of the links between them are displayed in Althusser's attempt to clarify the relations between the practices of capitalist society. As an example, he speaks about the reproduction of the relations of production – itself a precondition of the survival of the production process. For, 'As Marx said, every child knows that a social formation which did not reproduce the conditions of production at the same time as it produced would not last a year'.[18] This process

cannot be thought at the level of the firm, because it does not exist at that level in its real conditions... A moment's reflection is enough to be convinced of this: Mr. X, a capitalist, who produces woollen yarn in his spinning mill, has to 'reproduce' his raw material, his spinning machines, etc. But *he* does not produce them for his own production – other capitalists do. An Australian sheep farmer, Mr. Y, a heavy engineer producing machine tools Mr. Z, etc., etc. And Mr. Y and Mr. Z, in order to produce those products which are the conditions of the reproduction of Mr. X's conditions of production, also have to reproduce the conditions of their own production, and so on to infinity – the whole in proportions such that, on the national and even international markets, the demand for means of production (for reproduction) can be satisfied by the supply. In order to think this mechanism, which leads to a kind of 'endless chain,' it is necessary to follow Marx's 'global' procedure, and to study in particular the relations of the circulation of capital in Department I (production of means of production) and Department II (production of means of consumption), and the realisation of surplus value.[19]

The reproduction of the means of production depends upon two things. First, certain 'state apparatuses' such as the government, police, or army, may use violent means to keep the workers in their

---

[17] FM p.200.
[18] *Lenin, Philosophy and Other Essays*, trans. Ben Brewster (London, 1971) p.123. Hereafter abbreviated to L and P.
[19] L and P, p.124.

place.[20] But this is not only achieved by force, for there are also 'ideological state apparatuses', such as the education system, religion and the family, which maintain the *status quo* in more subtle ways.[21] Now, Althusser consigns state apparatuses to political practice, and ideological state apparatuses to ideological practice. He then suggests that the former can either directly create the conditions for the reproduction of the relations of production, presumably by quelling any sign of working class insubordination (i.e., a feature of economic practice depends upon political practice), or they can do so indirectly, by establishing a situation in which ideological state apparatuses can do their work (i.e., in which ideological practice determines economic practice). This set of relations is only roughly sketched, but it is possible to understand the idea underlying it. If it is against the interests of the working class to cooperate with capitalists, there are nevertheless two possible ways of persuading them to do so. They can either be forced, or they can be 'deluded' into thinking that it actually serves their own ends. Althusser's reason for assigning these strategies to different practices is, I think, that he believes that they achieve a single result (as far as economic practice is concerned) in radically different ways. Although the product is the same, the modes of production are separate.

Practices are therefore interdependent. But this account also indicates that an analysis of society in terms of practices might enable us to understand not only how states of affairs are maintained, but also how they change. We have seen that Althusser invokes certain aspects of political and ideological practice to explain the reproduction of the relations of production. But conversely, the failure of these mechanisms would explain the emergence of new production relations, which in turn would have consequences for other aspects of society. The model for this part of Marx's theory therefore seems to be a system in which an imbalance between two parts may lead to compensatory adjustments at other levels or may lead to a major reorganisation of the whole.

An account of society in terms of practices which may 'complement' or 'undermine' each other is therefore potentially able to provide both a social theory, and a theory of history, since it gives us a way of analysing the relations between practices at

[20] L and P, pp. 131–5.   [21] L and P, pp. 135–41.

a particular time and the conditions in which they change. According to Althusser, this model is the key to the Marxist concepts of contradiction and non-contradiction; for these are ideal types of the two ends of the spectrum of relations which can exist between practices. Practices are 'contradictory' when they 'grate' on each other, and non-contradictory when they 'support' one another. Although this is no more than a metaphorical description, it nevertheless serves to give some idea of what these relations are like. And to improve this understanding we must look to the only example Althusser provides: Lenin's discussion of the Russian Revolution.

Lenin wishes to explain why it was that although the 'peaceful mask' of capitalism had been torn off in all the countries of Western Europe by the end of the nineteenth century, and popular discontent was widespread, it was only in Russia that a successful revolution occurred.[22] He suggests that this was due to the fact that Russia was the 'weak link' in a 'collection of imperialist states', by virtue of the fact that it contained 'all the contradictions which were then possible within a single state'.[23] The explanation of the revolution is consequently traced to two sets of circumstances. The first are conditions within Russia, such as large-scale exploitation in cities, suburbs, mining districts, etc., the disparity between urban industrialisation and the medieval condition of the countryside, and the lack of unity of the ruling class. The second deals with the relation of Russia to the rest of the world, and includes the existence of an elite of Russians, exiled by the czar, who had become sophisticated socialists, as well as those aspects of foreign policy which played into the hands of the revolutionaries.

Althusser uses this case to support his claim that Marx held a complex view of social change, and did not regard it as the outcome of a single contradiction between the forces and the relations of production. He appeals to the differences between events in Russia and the other parts of Western Europe to show that while a contradiction between the forces and relations of production may be a necessary condition of a situation in which revolution is 'the task of the day', it is clearly not sufficient to bring about a revolution proper.[24]

[22] FM, pp.94–100.   [23] FM, p.95.
[24] FM, p.99.

If this contradiction is to become '*active*' in the strongest sense, to become a ruptural principle, there must be an accumulation of 'circumstances' and 'currents' so that whatever their origin and sense (and many of them will necessarily be paradoxically foreign to the revolution in origin and sense, or even its 'direct opponents') they '*fuse*' into a '*ruptural unity*' when they produce the result of the immense majority of the popular masses *grouped* in an assault upon a regime which its ruling classes are *unable to defend*.[25]

And then he claims that the list of circumstances above were among the factors needed to produce the revolution in Russia. Furthermore, these circumstances are said to be essentially heterogeneous, so that they cannot be seen as aspects of one large contradiction; each is a contradiction within a particular social totality.

If, as in this situation, a vast accumulation of contradictions comes into play *in the same court*, some of which are radically heterogeneous – of different origins, different sense, different *levels* and *points* of application – but which nevertheless 'merge' into a ruptural unity, we can no longer talk of the sole, unique power of the general contradiction.[26]

Althusser therefore concludes that Marx's concept of contradiction is inseparable from that of a social whole, and borrows a Freudian term to describe the relations between various states of affairs. Changes in social structure are said to be *overdetermined* by numerous contradictions.[27]

Even in such a brief survey of this notion of contradiction two things become clear. First, it is a relation which can hold between several different types of term. Until now we have considered practices within a society, and allowed that if these fail to complement each other they are said to be contradictory. But Althusser's example indicates that there can also be contradictions between aspects of one practice, such as the methods of production which are used in urban and in rural districts, between social groups, for example different factions of a ruling class, and between aspects of two societies, such as the contradictions thrown up by foreign policy. An analysis of contradictory practices can therefore be supplemented by an account of contradictions between smaller units. Althusser himself certainly takes this view.

[25] *Ibid.*   [26] FM, p.100.
[27] FM, p.101.

He says, for instance, that the conditions of a major contradiction are themselves the 'fusion' of an accumulation of contradictions.[28]

However, this approach holds dangers for him which become apparent when we try to discover what a contradiction is. The examples listed earlier suggest that it covers a vast variety of relations; for example the relation between capitalists and workers is said to be one of oppression, while that between factions of the ruling class might be competition. So, at anything other than an exceedingly general and metaphorical level, there is not a single set of criteria for a contradiction in the Marxist sense. In order to describe what is common to all instances of the concept it is necessary to talk in terms of relations within (or between) particular totalities which, when taken together, prompt social change. As such, the dialectic can easily become a teleological notion, covering any factors which turn out to contribute to some structural change in society. To avoid this, the theorist must presumably have various ideal types of *kinds* of contradictions in mind, on the basis of which he or she can generalise, and even predict. But since contradiction is the only source of social change in Althusser's account of the 'complex structured whole', it is important to bear its eclectic character in mind.

In this account Althusser has challenged the idea that radical social changes such as revolutions – which he treats as a blueprint for change in general – are the result of a single contradiction in society. He has pointed out that both our own experience and Marx's writings suggest that changes result from a disparate collection of circumstances which cannot be reduced to a single contradiction, but are jointly sufficient for a situation to become volatile. However, this is not intended to condemn us to the conclusion that changes in society are the chance results of unrelated factors. For all these states of affairs are said to be united within the complex whole. Althusser describes their unity in a variety of ways. 'The unity they *constitute* in this "fusion" into a revolutionary rupture, is *constituted by their own essence and effectivity*, by what they are, and according to the specific modalities of their action.'[29] First of all, contradictions can only be identified in the context of the whole, because it is only within it that states of affairs become incompatible with one another. Furthermore, the whole contains parts which are, as we have seen, more or less

---

[28] FM, p.98. [29] FM, p.100.

closely related. Thus, when he says that changes are 'over-determined' he has in mind a variety of factors, some more nearly connected than others, which all contribute to a single outcome. He lays particular stress on two consequences of this analysis, both of which are presented as advantages of Marx's theory. First, it allows that many kinds of circumstances can contribute to the course of events, and secondly it enables us to understand how these may combine to bring about dramatic and unexpected social changes which Althusser calls 'ruptures'.

Until now it has been assumed that social changes are determined by events which have the same status in the sense that they may all be conditions and consequences of each other. But this obviously raises the question of whether any primacy is to be accorded to economic practice. While the view which I earlier called crude materialism is not compatible with Althusser's general position, it would be remarkable if he were to relegate the economic aspects of society to exactly the same status as everything else. And indeed, he does give an account of the structure of the complex whole, and argues that it awards a certain primacy to economic practice 'in the last instance'.

This analysis is based on the works of Lenin and Mao, whose interpretation of the notion of contradiction Althusser adopts, on the grounds that it coincides with his own symptomatic reading of Marx. Every complex whole is therefore said to contain a principal contradiction and secondary contradictions. Each of these is said to have principal and secondary aspects. And finally, the contradictions within the whole are said to develop unevenly.[30] From what has already been said it is possible to gain a rough understanding of the second and third of these claims. Any features of a social situation which we pick out and identify as the terms of a contradiction may already be the result of a collection of further factors, some more important than others. So in this sense a contradiction has principal and secondary aspects. And the relative autonomy of certain factors within the whole allows the possibility of uneven development; for example an economic mode of production may run ahead of a legitimating ideology, or a scientific revolution may not lead to technological change. However, the first condition is the most important in Althusser's interpretation. He points out that a complex whole which contains

[30] FM, p.200.

principal and secondary contradictions will also contain relations of domination and subordination (since the factors forming the principal contradiction will dominate those forming the subordinate contradiction), and argues that the presence of these characteristics in a complex whole is not merely a contingent matter, but a necessary one.[31] Now it is certainly true that a complex whole *necessarily* contains relations of subordination and domination if the presence of principal and secondary contradictions within it is made into a defining characteristic. For this is to stipulate that Lenin's three criteria must be satisfied if a whole is to count as a complex one. Althusser seems to take this view when he argues that

The domination of one contradiction over the others cannot, in Marxism, be the result of a contingent distribution of different contradictions in a collection that is regarded as an object. In this complex whole 'containing' many contradictions we cannot 'find' one contradiction that dominates the others, as we might 'find' one spectator a head taller than the others in the grandstand at the stadium. Domination is not just an indifferent *fact*, it is a fact *essential* to the complexity itself.[32]

But as it stands, this declaration does not explain *why* we should accept these criteria, nor why Lenin's proposal is anything other than arbitrary. Nor does it immediately show us how this approach allots a special role to the economy, since the dominant contradiction of a society may be a feature of any practice at all, and may change with circumstances. These questions therefore demand attention. Althusser has a theoretical reason for adopting the views of Lenin and Mao. He says,

If every contradiction is a contradiction in a complex whole structured in dominance, this complex whole cannot be envisaged without its contradictions, without their basically uneven relations. In other words, each contradiction, each essential articulation of the structure, and the general relation of the articulations in the structure in dominance, constitute so many conditions of the existence of the complex whole itself. This proposition is of the first importance. For it means that the structure of the whole, and the 'difference' of the essential contradictions and their structure in dominance, is the very existence of the whole: that the 'difference' of the contradictions...is identical to the conditions of the existence of the complex whole. In plain terms this position implies that...the secondary contradictions are essential even to the existence of

[31] FM, p.201.   [32] *Ibid.*

a principal contradiction...that they really constitute its conditions of existence, just as the principal contradiction constitutes their condition of existence.[33]

For example, the relations of production are not pure phenomena of the forces of production. 'The superstructure is not the pure phenomenon of the structure, it is also its condition of existence.'[34] Furthermore, Althusser explains how it is that the economy can have some primacy within this structure. 'In the last instance' it determines the 'structure in dominance'.[35] The point of introducing this distinction between determination in the last instance and the structure in dominance is to combine the idea that the practices of which society is made up are mutually determining with the ultimate dominance of the economy.[36] But Althusser's own account does not make it clear how this is to be done. It is only in the work of his followers that a fuller analysis is to be found, which explains what is meant by 'determination in the last instance' and suggests what further reasons Althusser might offer for accepting Lenin's distinction between principal and secondary contradictions.

Until now I have presented Althusser's analysis of society as designed to explain social change by appealing to the notion of contradiction. We saw that this term was used very generally to describe various sorts of tension which arise in social practices, or between them, and which may provoke changes in the structure of society. However, at the other end of the scale these relations may complement each other, and thus be used to explain the stability of a particular form of social organisation. The way in which the economy determines the 'structure in dominance' in the last instance can most clearly be seen in the context of a stable society where practices are mutually supportive. I will therefore follow Althusser's associate, Etienne Balibar – who gives the clearest and fullest exposition of this idea – in discussing it with this sort of example in mind.[37]

Althusser's conception of a structure in dominance is based on the sense, which he attributes to Marx, that in each society one particular kind of interest appears to be central in determining the character of that society as a whole; for example, economic

---

[33] FM, p.205.   [34] *Ibid.*   [35] FM, p.111.   [36] FM, p.202.
[37] E. Balibar, 'The Basic Concepts of Historical Materialism' in *Reading Capital*, pp.199–309.

interests are uppermost in capitalist society, but during the Middle Ages religious concerns dominated social life. The aspect of society which is seen to be most important in this respect is called the dominant instance, and Althusser and his followers argue that it is determined in the last instance by the economy. That is to say, the economic practice of a society determines that some other aspect of it will be dominant in the structure of the society as a whole. This view is supported by a passage from the first volume of *Capital*, in which Marx answers the objection that his theory only applies to capitalist society.

My view...that the mode of production of material life dominates the development of social, political and intellectual life generally...is very true for our own times, in which material interests predominate, but not for the Middle Ages, in which Catholicism, nor for Athens and Rome where politics reigned supreme. In the first place it strikes one as an odd thing for anyone to suppose that those well-worn phrases about the Middle Ages and the ancient world are unknown to anyone else. This much, however, is clear, that the middle ages could not live on Catholicism, nor the ancient world on politics. On the contrary, it is the economic conditions of the time that explain why here politics and there Catholicism played the chief part. It requires but a slight acquaintance with the history of the Roman Republic, for example, to be aware that its secret history is the history of its landed property. On the other haʌd, Don Quixote long ago paid the penalty for imagining that knight errantry was compatible with all economic forms of society.[38]

This is the exegetical foundation for a conclusion which Balibar sums up as follows: 'In different structures the economy is determinant in that it determines which of the instances of the social structure occupies a determinant place.'[39]

However, even this bare summary raises two important questions. What is a dominant instance other than an aspect of society which appears intuitively important? And how does the economy determine which instance is to be dominant? As the answer to the first of these shows, the pair are closely linked; for there appear to be two kinds of criteria for identifying the dominant instance of a society, which are more or less explicitly mentioned in Althusser's work. On one hand, it is possible to pick out a dominant instance by its relationship with other aspects of

[38] K. Marx, *Capital* vol. 1, trans. S. Moore and E. Aveling (London, 1954) p.81n.
[39] RC, p.224.

a social structure. For although practices, and features of practices, are said to be mutually dependent, it is nevertheless possible that one may dominate the others in the sense that it is more efficacious in determining the character of other practices than they are in determining it.[40] This possibility is not openly discussed by Althusser, but it is certainly implied by his claim that some 'instances' of society are more autonomous than others. But while he indicates that there are such criteria for distinguishing between dominant and subordinate instances, Althusser pays far more attention to the relation between the dominant instance and economic practice, which itself constitutes a second sort of criterion for identifying the dominant instance. This relation is most clearly portrayed in the examples given by Balibar. First of all, it is assumed that in any mode of production where surplus value is not returned to the producers but is taken by other members of society, some justification of this distribution of wealth is required. In capitalist society the fetishism of commodities sustains the view that the accumulation of surplus value is a property of commodities themselves. But in other modes of production some external factor is needed to legitimate this arrangement; and Balibar claims that this is why certain political conditions, or a certain kinship structure, may be represented as a feature of the natural order of things, rather than being regarded as implied by a mode of production. For example, in feudal society products were not 'of themselves' the property of the ruling class, but became so in the light of various political practices. The *dominant* instance of a society is therefore that aspect of it which sustains the prevalent economic system by legitimating the way in which it produces and distributes wealth. Its domination resides in the fact that it keeps the economy going, without which the whole society would collapse, and in the fact that it thereby imposes certain restrictions on other practices. For if a particular form of social life is to be maintained, the practices of a society must not undermine the legitimating scheme embodied in the dominant instance.

The inspiration of this analysis is thus the underlying idea that any mode of production which redistributes wealth away from its producers will not survive unless it can be made to appear

[40] RC, p.106.

acceptable, and that certain modes of legitimation are particularly well-suited to certain modes of production. This is then used to explain both why societies contain a dominant instance, and how it is determined by economic practice. However, the first of these claims is still puzzling. For apart from Lenin's conviction that there is always a dominant instance at a time of social stability, and a dominant contradiction at a time of social change, Althusser gives us no reason to believe that there need only be *one* aspect of society which bears this relation to the mode of production. It is certainly true that Marx speaks of single practices as central to societies (as in the passage quoted earlier) and Althusser may well believe that as far as exegesis is concerned no more need be said. But if his aim is to justify as well as to interpret Marx's theory, the point becomes more pressing. For it seems that some assurance is required that societies have and must have this structure. Why, after all, should there not be a mode of production which is equally dependent on a variety of kinds of legitimation?

An analysis of social practices, and of their complementary and contradictory relations must take account, as we have seen, of many kinds of variables. But Althusser imposes one stringent limitation on the types that are admissible when he asserts that Marxist history is 'a process without a subject'. Out of this claim stem the most radical, and as far as our purposes are concerned, the most interesting aspects of his theory; for it is its 'subjectless' character which makes it so uncompromisingly holistic.

By 'the abolition of the subject' Althusser means the abolition of the intentional subject whose desires, motives, and beliefs are cited as the explanation of social events and states of affairs. And since persons are the primary *locus* of intentional properties, his main target is the traditional conception of individual agents, so central to individualism, which was discussed in Chapter III. Rather than being regarded as actors who make their own history, individuals are to be seen as the 'supports' of social practices who maintain and reproduce them. As Althusser puts it:

The structure of the relations of production determines the places and functions occupied and adopted by the agents of production, who are never anything more than the occupants of these places, insofar as they are the supports (*Träger*) of these functions. The true 'subjects' (in the sense of constitutive subjects of the process) are therefore not these occupants or functionaries, are not, despite all appearances, the 'obviousness' of the 'given' of naive anthropology, 'concrete individuals', 'real men' – *but the definition and distribution of these places and functions.*[41]

This is not to deny, of course, that individuals are causal subjects: they fill various social roles, engage in the work of production, and thereby bring about changes in the social world. But, in keeping with Marx's rejection of *homo oeconomicus*, their intentional properties are to be regarded as consequences, rather than causes, of social practice.

This conception of individuals as determined by social practice is familiar enough, but it remains to see how Althusser fills it out. First of all, because conditions vary from society to society, the social practices in which particular individuals engage will depend on time and place. This much is uncontentious, and provides a defence of the claim that the properties of individuals are not constant, so that – as Althusser puts it – each class has 'its' individuals, whose beliefs and behaviour are founded upon their experiences. However, Althusser also argues that, as well as the manifestations of subjecthood changing from society to society, the concept of subjecthood itself also changes. What it is to be an individual subject fluctuates from ideology to ideology.

Where only a single subject (such and such an individual) is concerned, the existence of the ideas of his belief is material in that *his ideas are his material actions inserted into material practices governed by material rituals which are themselves defined by the material ideological apparatus from which we derive the ideas of that subject*...It therefore appears that the subject acts in so far as he is acted by the following system:...Ideology existing in a material ideological apparatus, prescribing material practices governed by a material ritual, which practices exist in the material actions of a subject acting in all consciousness according to his belief.[42]

A central part of our view of individual agents is our conviction that there is an explanatory link between belief and action. But Althusser argues that this, too, is the fruit of practice:

The ideological representation of ideology is itself forced to recognise that every 'subject' endowed with a 'consciousness' and believing in the 'ideas' that his 'consciousness' inspires in him and freely accepts, must 'act according to his ideas', must therefore inscribe his own practice as

[41] RC, p.180.   [42] L and P, p.157.

a free subject in the actions of his material practice. If he does not do so, 'that is wicked'...In every case, the ideology of ideology thus recognises, despite its imaginary distortion, that the 'ideas' of a human subject exist in his actions, or ought to exist in his actions, and if that is not the case, it sends him other ideas corresponding to the actions (however perverse) that he does perform.[43]

Within bourgeois society the human individual is generally regarded as a subject with a certain range of properties including that of being a self-conscious agent. However, people's capacity for perceiving themselves in this way is not innate; it is acquired within a framework of established social practices which impose on them the role (*forme*) of a subject.[44] Each set of social practices not only determines the characteristics of the individuals who engage in it but also supplies them with a conception of the range of properties they can have, and of its limits. For example, individuals brought up in a truly Marxist society would presumably not regard themselves as the subjects of history, whereas those in bourgeois society believe that they are intentional agents.

How, though, does the complex whole of society make individuals in its own image? Althusser argues that our sense of ourselves as subjects is an effect of ideology, which

'acts' or 'functions' in such a way that it 'recruits' subjects among the individuals (it recruits them all) or 'transforms' the individuals into subjects (it transforms them all) by that precise operation which I have called hailing or *interpellation*, and which can be imagined along the lines of the most everyday polite (or other) hailing: 'Hey you there.'[45]

The 'precision' of this mechanism leaves something to be desired. But Althusser elaborates it a little, using the example of Christianity, where religious practice is said to 'hail' the individual and provide him with his status as a subject.

It [the subject] says: I address myself to you, a human individual...in order to tell you that God exists and that you are answerable to Him...This is your origin, you were created by God for all eternity, although you were born in the 1920'th year of our Lord! This is your place in the world! This is what you must do!...God thus defines himself as the Subject *par excellence*; he who is through himself for himself (I am that I am), he who interpellates his subject.[46]

[43] L and P, p.158.   [44] RJL, p.71.   [45] L and P, p.163.
[46] L and P, pp.165–6.

This case is supposed to show not only how Christianity works as an ideology, but how ideology works in general. Althusser denies the need for a more detailed account on the grounds that 'As the formal structure of all ideology is always the same, I shall restrict myself to a single example, one accessible to everyone, that of religious ideology, with the proviso that the same demonstration can be produced for ethical, legal, political, aesthetic ideology, etc.'[47]

I shall say more about this account of the role of ideology shortly. Before that it is worth reiterating Althusser's holistic view of the individual, and introducing an analogy which he takes from Marx. The concept of 'fruit', Marx says, is the product of various practices concerned with diet, agriculture and so on. In a comparable way, our concept of the individual must be seen as the conjuncture of the various practices which make up the complex whole.

Individuals are therefore not subjects, and if history is to be a process without a subject there must be no subjects short of the *ensemble* of practices itself. How, then, are classes to be analysed? These, too, are defined by their position in the whole, and by the opposed interests they have within it. They must be seen not as social groups constituted by individuals, but as positions constituted by the conflicting interests which are an integral part of a particular mode of production. To regard them as rival teams which are first constituted and *then* begin to play against each other is a serious mistake. Rather, they must be seen as sets of roles which, as soon as they exist, exploit one another and are thus engaged in the class struggle. Consequently, when we ask about the *autonomy* of classes within the complex whole we are not asking about their ability – or lack of it – to make choices, any more than we would ask if a force of production could choose. We are demanding to know whether they can function as independent variables in the explanations of events and states of affairs, or whether they are always dependent ones.

Althusser's abolition of the subject therefore commits him to an unequivocally holist account of social explanation. But it also has important consequences for the epistemological status of the resulting social theory, and much of the novelty of Marxism is said to arise from its break with traditional conceptions of knowledge.

47 L and P, p.165.

Absolute holism and its framework: Althusser   105

We have already seen how Althusser rejects the claim that individuals are intentional subjects, and argues instead that this self-perception is a result of ideological practice. He now launches a parallel attack on the idea that individuals are by nature the sort of creatures who can come to know things through their experience of the external world. Rather, knowledge is gained within the context of practices, which determine what a given individual knows and also contain certain standards as to what counts as knowledge. Thus, although we may say of individuals that they know this or that proposition, we can only explain this fact if we take into account the network of practices in which they live. Once again, the individual is not a suitable starting-point, and once again Althusser argues that there *is* no such starting-point. There is *no* subject of knowledge.

Nevertheless, 'knowledges' are products like any others, and are thus the results of certain processes of production, made up of the usual elements. They require labour, an object on which labour is expended, and a means of labouring, as well as involving the expenditure of labour *power* to transform the object of labour into the product, knowledge.[48] Althusser is emphatic that the means of production are just as essential to the fashioning of theoretical products as to something like shoemaking, which plainly requires leather, tools, etc., and he points out that the Marxist concept of labour is in this sense irreducibly material. Because it always involves raw materials and techniques it is always dependent upon a context, and is not to be thought of, in humanist vein, as an isolated expression of the essential creativity of human beings.[49]

Knowledge is therefore the result of a mode of production, and the product of a particular kind of practice. However, this has to be made compatible with Marx's claim that knowledge is produced in thought (it is a thought-object) a statement which seems to imply that it is, after all, produced by individuals. Althusser synthesises these two statements in the following way.

When Marx tells us that the production process of knowledge, and hence that of its object...takes place entirely in knowledge, in the 'head' or in thought, he is not for one second falling into an idealism of consciousness, mind or thought, for the '*thought*' we are discussing here

48 RC, p.58.   49 RC, pp.172-3.

is not a faculty of a transcendental subject or absolute consciousness confronted by the world as matter: nor is this thought a faculty of a psychological subject, although human individuals are its agents. This thought is the historically constituted system of an *apparatus of thought*, founded on and articulated to natural and social reality. It is defined by the system of real conditions which make it, if I may dare to use such a phrase, a *determinate mode of production* of knowledges. As such it is constituted by a structure which combines the type of object (raw material) on which it labours, the theoretical means of production available (its theory, its method, and its technique, experimental or otherwise) and the historical relations (both theoretical, ideological and social) in which it produces.[50]

This is not to deny that individuals are able to think, that they have ideas, build theories, etc. But once again it is to deny that they can do this by virtue of their intrinsic properties as individuals. The object on which an individual expends mental labour is never a 'pure representation', any more than he can transform it into knowledge just like that. Both the problems which individuals fix upon, and the methods they employ to solve them, are part of their theoretical heritage, so to speak, enshrined in the practices of which they are the supports. Thus theory and practice cannot be separated. For even the most primitive practices are dependent upon a certain amount of theory, and even the most 'theoretical' activities can only take place within practices.[51]

Now the structures of practices are not always the same, but rather depend upon the various elements of the production processes they contain. Nevertheless, there must be some feature which distinguishes the production of *knowledge* from that of political slogans, for example; and we have to try to understand how the real object is transformed into the thought object. Althusser faces this question, but warns that it has to be carefully formulated if it is to illuminate the process of the production of knowledges. In particular, we must avoid giving an ideological answer.[52] Broadly, practices, propositions, beliefs, and so forth, are ideological when they present a state of affairs in such a way as to render it attractive or self-evident to a specific audience. They therefore cannot be fully understood if they are taken at face value, and an investigator must find out what social situations sustain and are reflected in them. 'It is not their real conditions of

[50] RC, p.41.   [51] RC, pp.58–9.   [52] RC, p.15.

existence, their real world, that "men" "represent to themselves" in ideology, but above all, it is their relation to those conditions of existence which is represented to them there.'[53] Furthermore, the investigator must uncover the questions to which a set of ideological propositions are the answers. This last piece of methodological advice is important, because it reveals a central feature of Althusser's definition of ideology. Ideologies do not just appear in societies; their function is to legitimate practices, and they are formulated for this purpose. Because they are designed to justify certain propositions, the questions they ask are formulated in such a way as to prompt the desired answers. In short, they do not begin with a question and seek an answer; they rather start with an answer and devise a corresponding question.

This self-sustaining quality is said to be exemplified by current epistemologies. Empiricist theories of knowledge, for example, are presented as a legitimating ideology for individualist social theories which in turn are part of a bourgeois outlook, and are said to pose questions designed to justify the individual as knower and as agent. But this epistemology itself is parasitic upon other practices, which serve the same ideological function. Indeed, Althusser claims to identify the origins of such an attitude in the law; he suggests that the ideological notion of the legal subject as the owner of property was taken over by Kant and Descartes and transformed into the philosophical categories of subject and object.[54] A serious attempt to understand the relation between the real object and the thought object must therefore avoid the trap of giving an ideological answer, and this in turn demands that questions about the character of the relation should be open-ended; they must not presuppose any one conclusion.

Since ideology works in a mysterious way, it is not easy to see what would count as meeting such a standard, but it is clear that Althusser himself does not succeed. For while he goes to some lengths to avoid formulating a question which presupposes the distinction between subject and object, he is frankly concerned to provide an answer (and hence a question) which will be compatible with the claim that social changes are overdetermined by the complex whole, and which will therefore embody a particular view of the production of knowledge. To this end, he argues that we must shun the temptation to think in terms of specifying conditions

[53] L and P, p.154.   [54] L and P, pp.93–4.

which *guarantee* knowledge, because this approach assumes a subject for whom it is guaranteed.[55] Instead we must ask in more impersonal terms about the 'mechanism' by which the real object is 'appropriated' and becomes the thought object. The power of this move lies in the implication that a 'mechanism' is not a feature of a subject, but of a structure. Putting the problem in these terms already suggests that criteria of knowledge only arise within some set of related concepts, which in turn are connected to certain activities. Althusser's question therefore paves the way for his view that a corpus of knowledge is the outcome of practices.

To present these views clearly is exceedingly difficult, and Althusser's own account of them is far from luminous. However, to get a better grasp of the holism they embody, it is helpful to view them in a more critical spirit. Since it first appeared, Althusser's work has attracted a great deal of attention, and his opponents have focussed in particular on his holist stance. Some of their objections are easily disposed of, but others reveal serious lacunae and inconsistencies which require to be dealt with. They present both a problem and a challenge; for any theory which overcame them would vindicate a form of holistic social explanation of a power hitherto unaccepted.

Althusser's holism consists, as we have seen, in an attempt to explain *all* social phenomena in terms of certain aspects of social structure, at the expense of explanations which appeal to the properties of individual subjects. His abolition of the subject carries with it the demise of the individual as the locus of knowledge and agency, and places him in a position where, as we saw, there can be no question of compromise with individualism. For rather than being the *locus* of action, choice, etc., the individual is to be seen as a 'conjuncture' of social practices; each person's intentional properties can be 'explained away' as the result of constraints imposed upon them by the structured whole. It is important to recognise that this view is not incompatible with the mention of individuals in explanations; it is only incompatible with the mention of individual subjects. Althusser actually says that an ideal explanation would map out the relations between different factors down to and including individuals, and thus outlines a programme for a perfect social theory which would account for the parts played by individuals in social organisation and change.[56]

Although Althusser's interpretation of Marx cannot, in the nature of things, live up to its own ideal of a theory which has *no* starting point, it follows the life-cycle of persons who are born into a web of relations and social conventions in starting out from a complex whole made up of practices. Rather than concerning itself with the way in which the properties of this structure emerge from its components, it takes the structure as given and asks how it reproduces itself and changes. The properties of *individuals* emerge from the many aspects of the complex whole.

Having seen how Althusser presents this idea, and the extent to which he develops its consequences, it remains to ask whether it is coherent. To make sense of it one would first of all have to distinguish between, and learn to identify, the various kinds of structural constraints which form individuals and social groups into the 'supports' of the complex whole. Many of the dichotomies traditionally employed in this area – for example between constraints operating through reasons and constraints due to other factors – are formulated with individual subjects in mind, and so do not apply, while others, which were originally intended to apply to only some properties of individuals and collectives, must bear extra weight. Since individuals are said to be altogether determined, constraints must be found to explain all their actions and intentions. Their opportunities, their *perception* of their opportunities, and their *choices* among their opportunities must all be determined by the complex whole, as must the fact that a ruling class opts for a particular ideology, and the fact that it opts for *any* justificatory ideology. For the theorist must be able to 'translate' with confidence an 'everyday' account of social events, into a suitable subjectless form.

There is obviously no *a priori* objection to such a procedure, and it would be naive to insist that a social theory must accord with our intuitive understanding of the social world any more than physical theory must. But many of Althusser's critics have roundly asserted that it is neither feasible nor desirable.

Of these, some have quarrelled with his view that individuals are determined by practices on the grounds that, as Lukes puts it, any theory built on such a foundation fails to deal with the

[56] RC, p.66.

central problem of the relation between structure (i.e. the constraints on actors) and agency (i.e. the freedom of agents).[57] But, put like this, the objection misses its mark. For Althusser does deal with this distinction – though not in a way Lukes can accept – by denying its validity. Structure and agency do not have to be reconciled, because the latter is only an ideological appearance.

This question-begging objection, which assumes a mutual dependence between individual agents and social practices and then upbraids Althusser for failing to take account of it, is often made. One author, for example, dismisses Althusser's view as 'absurd and extreme' on the grounds that

As a philosopher, Althusser tries to resolve conceptually what are questions for empirical investigation: the *degree* to which particular social figurations constrain individual people, and the *degree* to which individuals' actions can have effects upon the particular figurations in which they are caught up. Althusser's writings lack all the subtlety of the conception of the relationship between acting, thinking individuals and structured processes of change...or of Elias's account of the relationship between social control and self-control in the civilising process.[58]

These objections do not cut any ice; but there are nevertheless grounds for complaint. Among them is the fact that Althusser himself has difficulty in applying his theory to his own exposition of Marx's work. Throughout his discussion, terms such as 'individual' or 'person' appear in quotation marks, to indicate that they are only convenient figures of speech, not to be confused with the subjects of bourgeois ideology. But he refers without any apparent qualms to 'Marx's great achievement', to 'What Marx did', 'What Lenin saw', and so on. The fathers of Marxism are treated as subjects, and their names are not encircled by warning quotation marks. Admittedly, explaining their achievements is not part of Althusser's project, and he might therefore be excused for failing to indicate the specific historical conjuncture from which Marxism arose. But since it has proved notoriously difficult for determinists to account for the emergence of new and revolutionary ideas, it would surely be wise of Althusser to show how he proposes to do it. What is needed, as one of his followers has

[57] S. Lukes, 'Power and Structure' in *Essays in Social Theory* (London, 1977).
[58] S. Mennell, *Sociological Theory: Uses and Unities* 2nd edn (Walton-on-Thames, 1980) pp.90–1.

pointed out, is an account of theories which deals with changes 'at the level of the limits and consequences of the epistemological configuration they represent', rather than at the level of individuals.[59] Shifts from one 'problematic' to another, such as that from classical political economy to Marxism, must be explained so that 'later developments are determined by the structure of the ideological problematic from which they break, or the scientific problems which they recast'.[60] However, this is only a manifesto, and unless it can be implemented Althusser will have failed in his task of rendering Marx intelligible through Marxist philosophy. For the philosophy will have proved too weak to solve what is, after all, a familiar and pervasive problem for Marxists.

Once doubt has been cast on the consistency of Althusser's interpretation of Marx, it is natural to probe what is perhaps the most vulnerable aspect of his theory more deeply: his account of the role and character of ideological practice. As we have seen, the various ideological state apparatuses of a society are allotted the formidable task of constituting individual subjects, who then reproduce the practices which make up the structured totality of society. And as one of Althusser's commentators reminds us, 'Not only is there no special reason to believe that the subjects constituted and distributed by these mechanisms should be constituted so as to "understand" the mechanisms by which they are constituted but, on the contrary, it is a condition of operation of many of the mechanisms that they are not understood by the subjects they "constitute".'[61] This account gives rise to two questions, both of them large and difficult: first, how do ideological state apparatuses (ISAs) constitute individuals; and second, how can Althusser justify his claim that his theory escapes the tentacles of ideology and tells us how the world really is? I shall consider his attempts to deal with these in turn.

At the heart of Althusser's work is a desire to understand how modern societies reproduce themselves – how, for example, the vast and complex structures of modern capitalist states are maintained – and he implicitly divides this process into two connected parts. On the one hand a society must reproduce

[59] Keith Tribe, 'On the Production and Structuring of Scientific Knowledges', *Economy and Society* 2 (1973) p.470.
[60] *Ibid.*, p.472.
[61] Ted Benton, *Philosophical Foundations of the Three Sociologies* (London, 1977) p.176.

various roles – there must be slots for postmen, steelworkers, parents and civil servants – and on the other hand it must produce people to fill them. However, these requirements do not divide neatly between practices. The reproduction of jobs for steel-workers and the reproduction of steelworkers as such are at least in part features of economic practice, just as the reproduction of lawyers is part of politico-legal practice. But to fill a material role such as that of a steelworker or a lawyer, an individual must have been subjected to numerous other ISAs. Schools, families, newspapers, unions and so on all contribute to people's sense of themselves as agents with unique characters and life-plans.

The feature of Althusser's view that repels his liberal critics is his neglect of what they take to be a central distinction between the essential and contingent properties of individuals. As we saw in Chapter III, that a person does a particular job, lives in a particular town or is a vegetarian is usually regarded as a contingent fact about them. Even their stormy temperament or compulsive generosity could have been different. But the properties which make people into agents, such as their ability to exercise choice, to act on their intentions and so forth, are essential. Without them we should not be who we are; we should not be recognisable as normal adult humans at all. As we also found earlier, it is far from easy to specify exactly what being an autonomous agent *actually* consists in, although we have a firm conception of a kind of ideal type – someone moved by the pure light of reason who ponders the evidence before them and makes considered, unconstrained decisions. In life, however, the light of reason is dusty and obscured, and it is unclear how far this ideal type can help us to explain the course of our social existence. Partly as a response to this we distinguish between what we regard as essential *capacities* of humans and the question of how, or whether, they are exercised.

Althusser's view exploits this uncertainty over whether our conception of agency can carry much explanatory weight. He believes not only that our particular desires, expectations and values are to be explained by the structured wholes in which we live. The very line we draw between the contingent and essential properties of individuals is also the fruit of the same totalities, so that the traditional role of the distinction itself is abolished. And yet there is no special ideological practice which gives us the idea of it. Rather, it is embodied in all the ISAs of capitalist society, so that we learn it in the course of learning what it is to be a parent, a democrat, a black, a steelworker, or a councillor. Ideological practice does not constitute subjects as such, but *particular* subjects who have the belief that all subjects share some traits in common.

A persuasive account of ideological practice would have to begin by showing how this is done, and here Althusser's account is extremely weak. For his concept of 'interpellation' fails to explain the mechanism by which subjects are constituted, and is really no more than a redescription of its own result. All individuals are subjects, so all have by definition been interpellated. But how? And why does the process never fail? Furthermore, the claim that ISAs serve to legitimate and maintain the delicate balance of power within a structured totality needs to be elaborated, and its limits explored. When a society is stable, for instance, do all its ISAs fulfil their legitimating function, or do some work against the interests of the dominant classes of the society? By speaking of 'Ideological State Apparatuses', with their resonance of central control, Althusser implies that they are a unified set of institutions, in the service of a single mode of production. Yet his view that capitalist societies contain several overlapping modes of production and a number of classes and sections of classes, clearly demands something more complicated. The dominance of the dominant mode must be legitimated. But so must the subsidiary places of other modes and classes, despite their conflicting interests. There must be ISAs capable of reproducing the dominated classes of society. And at the same time their influence must be bounded by other, dominant ISAs. Some of Althusser's critics have pointed out that this monolithic conception of the role of ideology cannot account for the vast variety of 'ideological universes' found in modern capitalist states, some conformist and others overtly subversive.[62] If the claim that they all legitimate the existing order is to be more than a dogma it must be refined, and Althusser's work offers no suggestion as to how this is to be done.

An analysis of interpellation and legitimation which would underpin the central claim that subjects are constituted by ideology is thus striking for its absence. It then seems natural to ask how else the claim could be established. A different approach might aim to show that our perception of ourselves as intentional subjects

[62] *Ibid.*

has not always existed, and might then suggest that it arises as a feature of capitalist ideology. Althusser does not attempt such an argument but his sole example – a glancing reference to Foucault's studies of asylums and clinics – suggests that he might have some sympathy with it.[63] For somewhat like Althusser, Foucault defends a 'discursive determinism' which looks to a wide range of institutions and academic disciplines as the determinants of conceptions of agency. But again, Althusser's own account of the way in which intentional subjects are constituted by practices is undeveloped, and quite unsatisfactory as it stands.

These criticisms, which focus on what has been left undone rather than on what has been done, are inevitably inconclusive. For while they indicate how complicated and taxing it would be to build inside the scaffolding erected by Althusser, they do not show either that the building would stand or that it is doomed to collapse. In this respect they contrast with another set of objections, which point to ambiguities in the claims Althusser has actually made; and one of the most pertinent of these concerns his account of ideology. This is intended, as we saw, to counter explanations of social phenomena grounded in a theory of human nature: there are no essential human traits of interest to social theorists since subjects are constituted by the structured totality. But unless some assumptions are made about what people are like, it is not clear why communist societies contain ideologies at all. This criticism is forcefully made by Connolly, in the course of a discussion of structuralist theories, of which he takes Althusser's to be a prime example:

My charge is this: without an anthropological dimension in theory, it is inexplicable why the role bearers require ideology to bear the roles imposed by capitalism; with such an anthropology, the view that theory is not and cannot be made available to participants in ways that influence their future conduct must be revised profoundly. Structural theory does not eliminate, rather it suppresses, the anthropological dimension. And once the suppressed premise is exposed, structural theorists must re-engage the very issues they have sought to expunge from theory – issues such as the nature of human subjects; the relation between individual subjects and intersubjectivity; the structural limits to the emergence of self-consciousness; the connection between consciousness and political practice; and the moral inhibitions to both social control and revolutionary action.[64]

---

[63] RC, p.103.

[64] W. E. Connolly, *Appearance and Reality in Politics* (Cambridge, 1981) p.50.

One of the two complaints aired in this passage has already been discussed – the incredulous observation that we cannot view people as role-bearers who lead complicated lives in modern industrial societies and simultaneously regard them as determined. The other, however, is less commonplace. By allotting such a major place to ideological practice, Althusser supposes that people must somehow be cajoled, duped or persuaded into roles which do not reflect their true interests. In order for a capitalist mode of production to perpetuate itself, for example, a majority of capitalists and workers alike must fail to comprehend it. But why should this be so? Only because it is assumed that if people understood the system in which they were involved they would not put up with it, and it would not go on. But this is to assume that humans have a natural capacity to recognise and reflect on their interests, and that they will only stand so much injustice.

As a rebuttal of Althusser's account of the relation between individuals and structured totalities, this objection is incomplete. Ideologies *may* be needed to neutralise 'natural' human characteristics which are prior to all practices. But might they not also serve to overcome properties of the individual members of a society which are themselves the *result* of other social practices? If this were so, the existence of ideologies could be explained without resorting to an 'anthropological dimension'. Furthermore, an Althusserean who faces Connolly's criticism directly will surely reply that there is no question of individuals who have certain 'real interests' being 'duped' by ideology; to talk in this way is to revert to the very problematic Marx was striving to transcend. The function of ideological practice is not to 'deceive' ready-made subjects, but to constitute individuals as subjects. So although a different totality might produce subjects who were neither exploiters nor exploited, such individuals cannot be produced within capitalist societies. For they would have to have escaped the very apparatuses which constitute subjects, and thus would not *be* subjects at all.

This is a strong answer to the question in hand, but it releases a sea of epistemological troubles. First, as we have already noticed, Althusser's account must somehow explain the enormous variety of beliefs and judgments, many of them damaging to the *status quo*, that are found in capitalist societies (and others, for that matter). For example, if the only way to be a subject is to be constituted by the existing ISAs, how are we to explain the fact that a theorist such as Connolly is so convinced of the necessity of intentional subjecthood, while Althusser views it as a contingency? Did the ISAs slip up in Althusser's case? He might perhaps attribute the incompleteness of his account to the fact that he is a 'bourgeois' subject, who can only glimpse an alternative view of the individual; but this defence is still a problem, for even a glimpse suggests that the ISAs of the capitalist totality may be more or less effective, and this variation will have to be explained. Furthermore, what I have presented as the Althusserean reply to Connolly emphasises the claim that ISAs constitute subjects, at the expense of the view that they legitimate a mode of production. The reply, as I have imagined it, turns away Connolly's suggestion that ISAs somehow 'persuade' people into views and roles which do not reflect their own interest, on the grounds that these apparatuses constitute subjects rather than manipulating them. But social practices only need legitimating if there is some chance that they may be rejected. So it seems that this is a further reason for Althusser to allow that the process of constitution may be more or less successful. On the face of it, two lines of defence seem to be open to him. One alternative is to distinguish the constitution of individuals as intentional subjects who reason, choose and decide, from their constitution as capitalists, workers or lumpenproletariat, and to argue that it is the particular roles of a society which give rise to the need for legitimation. But it is unlikely that Althusser would welcome such an option because, as we saw, he is anxious to reject this very distinction. The other alternative is to claim that the very constitution of individuals as intentional subjects serves to legitimate capitalist modes of production, for only if individuals perceive themselves as free agents will these alienating arrangements seem tolerable. The constitution of subjects, and the simultaneous constitution of the occupants of particular roles would then both be seen as forms of legitimation. This approach to the problem looks the more promising of the two, but it prompts an absolutely central question: what is the status of Althusser's claims about the relation between individuals and structured totalities? How does he know – or how do *we* know – that they are right?

Althusser's answer to this most pressing query has developed in the course of his work. Early on, he was anxious to combine the view that our beliefs about the social world are determined by the structured whole with the claim that historical materialism has achieved the status of a science, a body of knowledge which gives us a true account of the world. Later, however, he conceded that this attempt had been unsuccessful, and his earlier rigorous separation of science and ideology misguided.[65] If we are constituted as subjects by the totalities we inhabit, then our beliefs about the divide between science and ideology (Althusser's included) will be determined too, and we cannot expect to arrive at an impartial, objective view of it. Whereas Marx is usually thought to have envisaged a classless society in which people will no longer be deluded by false consciousness, Althusser has posited a determinism so strong as to be inescapable. A classless society would no doubt constitute subjects who (like Miss Beale and Miss Buss), would be different from us, but they would be constituted nonetheless, and could not know that their own conviction of being unexploited was not mistaken.

In his later work, however, Althusser modified his account of the distinction between science and ideology, a shift which has had important consquences for his analysis of the relation between individuals and practices. For his more recent view suggests that we cannot expect to gain untainted 'knowledge' of ourselves and our relation to social practices, so that the claim that individuals are not subjects must be assessed, like its competitors, by appeal to various kinds of criteria. Some of these, such as consistency, will be internal to the theory, while others will be decided from a more general conception of what social theories are supposed to achieve.

Whether it is possible to assess Althusser's view of the individual subject without implicitly reinstating it, remains to be seen. Yet some attempt at assessment must surely be made. One relatively straightforward approach to this task consists in trying to refine the theory through use – to discover, by applying it to specific problems, whether it can be consistently employed and what explanations it can yield.

It is this project which has been pursued with great tenacity by Nicos Poulantzas, who has applied Althusser's general theory to a specific case. For further elucidation of the way in which this form of holistic theory actually functions I shall therefore turn to Poulantzas' work, aiming to explicate and assess the absolute holism to which he is committed.

[65] L. Althusser, 'Elements of Self-Criticism' in *Essays in Self-Criticism*, trans. G. Locke (London, 1976). See especially pp.119–25.

V

The framework applied: Poulantzas

Of the various attempts that have been made to apply Althusser's principles, by far the most wholehearted and discerning is the work of Nicos Poulantzas, who offered both an account of the state in capitalist societies and an analysis of what he saw as one of its exceptional forms – fascism. The justice of his interpretation of the fascist state has been, and is, fiercely disputed, and I will not discuss it.[1] For its contours are set by Poulantzas' more general conception of the state, and it is here that he is most explicit in trying to put Althusser's theory to work. In order to understand his project and judge its success, it is important to grasp the problem Poulantzas sets himself: What question is he trying to answer? What does he want to explain? However, the complexity of his task is such that it cannot readily be summarised in a few words. Rather than contenting himself with a specific and clearly-defined puzzle, Poulantzas aims to give a broad account of the capitalist state, which will show what it is and what it does by revealing its connections with the various instances of the social whole. By delineating its links with the various economic and ideological structures of society on the one hand and with the class struggle on the other, he hopes to cast light on its constitution and character.[2]

The impetus for this undertaking derives from a lacuna in traditional Marxist theory – the fact that while the founding fathers acknowledged the importance of the state, their account of it as the tool of the ruling class is misleading. Poulantzas frankly

[1] See Jane Caplan, 'Theories of Fascism: Nicos Poulantzas as Historian', *History Workshop* 3 (1977) pp.83–100.

[2] This analysis has excited much discussion. See the works by Miliband and Laclau cited in this chapter, and also S. Clarke, 'Marxism, Sociology and Poulantzas' Theory of the State', *Capital and Class* 2 (1977) 1–31; Stuart Hall, 'Nicos Poulantzas: State, Power, Socialism', *New Left Review* 119 (1980) pp.60–9; Anthony Giddens, *A Contemporary Critique of Historical Materialism* (London, 1981) ch. IX.

sets out to ameliorate this condition with an interpretation which will accommodate the state's ability to curb as well as foster the interests of a ruling class while remaining true to the fundamental tenets of Marxism. This is then used as a basis for understanding the various *forms* of the capitalist state, and the transitions from one to another. The result, however, is not a 'theory of the state', an account of such generality as to be applicable to all societies at all times. Because he believes that the 'political instance', which in capitalist societies can be identified as the state, is a function of its relations with the other instances of the structured whole, Poulantzas concludes that there can be no such theory. The instances and their relations are subject to a degree of variation which would make it anachronistic even to posit a universal phenomenon called 'the state'. Poulantzas therefore confines his attention to capitalist societies, which he regards as sufficiently alike to be the subject-matter of a single theory.

As a means, therefore, of getting a firmer and more detailed grip on the kind of holism which Althusser and his followers have espoused, I shall begin by outlining the theory of capitalist states that Poulantzas has developed. I shall then enquire, in a more critical spirit, how successful his application of Althusser's absolute holism has been, and how much explanatory weight the resulting theory can be made to bear.

Poulantzas' theory is formulated, as I have said, in opposition to the conventional Marxist wisdom that the state is the tool of the ruling class. But his hostility to this view can be traced to the more general antipathy to voluntarism which we have already examined in Althusser's work, and which, according to Poulantzas, underlies the traditional Marxist account. For the designation of the state as 'a tool' is said to imply that it is an inert object which can be moulded and manipulated by the ruling class; and this in turn is said to carry the misleading connotation that the ruling class has a 'will'.

This school ultimately sees in the state the product of a subject, usually of the dominant-class/subject, whose mere tool of domination, manipulable at will, it is. The unity of this state is hence related to a presupposed unity of the 'will' of the dominant class with regard to which the state presents no autonomy.[3]

---

[3] Poulantzas, *Political Power and Social Classes*, trans. Timothy O'Hagan (London, 1975) pp.256–7. Hereafter abbreviated to PP and SC.

These assumptions are criticised for having various unfortunate consequences; but most of all, they belong to an approach which Poulantzas, following Althusser, labels 'historicist'. Its distinguishing characteristics are first the view that a class is partly constituted by the perceptions of its members, and second the belief, held either tacitly or openly, that the passage of history is marked by the growth of class consciousness, until a point in the future when an enlightened proletariat will be able to grasp its real interests and make its own history. This, however, is said to be nothing more than a scantily concealed voluntarism. If we are to attribute to social classes the capacity to perceive their interests, we shall have to analyse this property. We shall have to ask, for example, in what conditions classes recognise their interests and how observers can be sure that they have done so. And once we start such an enquiry, Poulantzas claims, we shall be dragged away from the objective definition of classes, back into individualist accounts of the perceptions and intentions of their members. The crux of this argument is the contention that it is impossible to attribute consciousness of its interests to a class (even to the revolutionary proletariat), without interpreting this notion in terms of the intentional properties of its members. What, after all, could such consciousness be, other than the beliefs and desires of various individuals? Since Poulantzas insists on an objective analysis of classes, and since he assumes that a satisfactory definition ought to characterise all classes without exception, he rejects historicism on the grounds that it has failed to escape from the problematic of individualism.

Whatever one thinks of this judgment, it is not immediately obvious that it entails the rejection of the more specific claim that the state is the tool of the ruling class; for the latter makes no explicit mention of a class's consciousness of its interests, real or otherwise. But Poulantzas argues that the attribution of the power to manipulate to the ruling class elevates it to the status of a subject – an agent who *does* things – and thereby reintroduces the idea of collective intensions which cry out for individualist explanation. As evidence of the difficulty of eschewing individualism he criticises a number of attempts to elaborate a conception of the state as the tool of the ruling class which *are* individualist. Even at their most sophisticated these are based on the observation that individuals who hold senior government posts and individuals who run major businesses often have certain things in common. As Miliband explains,

The assumption which is at work here is that a common social background and origin, education, connections, kinship and friendship, a similar way of life, result in a cluster of common ideological and political positions and attitudes, common values and perspectives. There is no necessary unanimity of views among the people in question and there may be fairly deep differences between them on this or that issue. But these differences occur within a specific and fairly narrow conservative spectrum. This being the case, it is to be expected, so the argument goes, that those who run the state apparatus should, at the very least, be favourably disposed towards those who own and control the larger part of the means of economic activity, that they should be much better disposed toward them than towards any other interest or class, and that they should seek to serve the interests and purposes of the economically dominant class, the more so since those who run the state power are most likely to be persuaded that to serve these interests and purposes is also, broadly speaking, to serve the 'national interest' or 'the interests of the nation as a whole'.[4]

While Poulantzas allows that the sort of research designed to sustain this view has some limited use,[5] he first of all objects that it does not bear out the factual claim that government officials and leading capitalists belong to an identifiable group. 'In point of fact, the hegemonic function has often been distinct from the *governing* class or function, and is so today in certain social formations.'[6] And in any case, this sort of information will hardly prove the point in question; for while it is true enough that capital can influence the filling of government posts, the formation of foreign policy and so on, this simply shows that the state is swayed by an interest group which may be one among many. It does not show that it always favours one interest – in fact the contrary seems to be true. Furthermore, it does *not* show that these are *class* interests, any more than the enumeration of cases shows that the government systematically protects the interests of what Poulantzas calls the hegemonic function of capital. To sustain the more general claims one would first need to have a systematic account of the class structure of a society which showed that the interests promoted

---

[4] R. Miliband, *Marxism and Politics* (Oxford, 1977) p.69.
[5] N. Poulantzas, *Classes in Contemporary Capitalism*, trans. David Fernbach (London, 1975) p.182. Hereafter abbreviated to C in CC.
[6] C in CC, p.183.

by the state were in fact those of the ruling class. Still more important, one would then need an account of the state as the sort of thing over which capital could exercise power – a set of institutions with no autonomy of their own.[7]

This attack on the argument for what I have called the traditional Marxist account of the state begins by taking it on its own terms. Even if it is agreed that a study of the aspirations, the jobs, the education and social background of certain individuals will elucidate the character of the relation between the ruling class and the state, the results are still far from decisive. But it quickly develops into the full-scale criticism of this approach that one would expect from a follower of Althusser. Rather than trying to explain the capitalist state as an outcome of the actions of individual and collective subjects, Poulantzas argues that it should be seen in the light of a general view of social structures, classes, and their relations. He then takes this brief to heart, and sets himself to provide an analysis of the state that avoids a formidable list of errors. First and foremost, it must not be voluntarist, and must therefore eschew any hint of historicism. Second, it must avoid economism. Third, it must elucidate the relation between the state and the ruling class. And finally, it must remedy the common mistake of making the class struggle peripheral to the workings of the state. (The importance of this last condition will emerge as we discuss Poulantzas' own approach, but it is initially justified in his work by an appeal to Marx's and Engels' claim that the class struggle is the motor of history.)[8]

Aiming, then, to avoid both voluntarism and economism, Poulantzas adopts Althusser's conception of society as a whole structured in dominance. Because agents are seen merely as the supports of this structure, their intentional properties do not enter into social explanation; and because its various components are interdetermined, the economic sphere does not have the straightforward primacy that economism requires. Instead, the totality itself is said to contain three instances – political, economic and ideological – one of which is dominant; and the identity of the dominant instance is in turn determined 'in the last instance' by the character of the economic mode of production. Poulantzas, like

---

[7] See Claus Offe and Volker Ronge, 'Theses on the Theory of the State', *New German Critique* 6 (1975) pp.139–47.
[8] PP and SC, ch. 1.

Althusser, believes that this arrangement remains constant and applies to all societies, but he argues that the more specific relations between instances vary with time and place. In some cultures, for example, the political may be largely determined by the economic, whereas in capitalist societies it is relatively autonomous. And even within a single formation the relations between instances are forever changing.

Societies are thus seen as made up of three interconnected structures, each of which is seen as a mode of production, transforming raw materials into commodities. But of course they each depend upon the existence of individuals who carry out the tasks necessary for the survival and perpetuation of society. To take an obvious case, modern manufacturing industries can only go on so long as there are capitalists and workers. So it is important to ask how these role-bearers are to be characterised in relation to the whole structured in dominance. In Poulantzas' view, this whole has the effect of dividing people up into classes: any mode of production 'requires' the existence of people who do jobs of various sorts, and who, by virtue of their roles, have implacably opposed interests.

Social class is a concept which shows the effects of the ensemble of structures, of the matrix of a mode of production or a social formation on the agents which constitute its supports: this concept reveals the effect of the global structure in the field of social relations. In this sense, if class is indeed a concept, it does not designate a reality which can be placed in the structures: it designates the effect of an ensemble of given structures, an ensemble which determines social relations as class relations.[9]

In addition to structures, therefore, there are also classes, and Poulantzas is anxious to keep the two categories apart – a desire which is particularly clear in his discussion of the relations which bind entities of each type. On the one hand, structures are marked by being more or less contradictory, due either to the strains of uneven development, or to the fact that societies usually contain several, overlapping modes of production. Classes, on the other hand, are related in a quite different way, since they are engaged in struggle at the economic, political and ideological levels.[10]

[9] PP and SC, pp.67–8.
[10] See R. W. Connell, 'A Critique of the Althusserean Approach to Class', *Theory and Society* 8 (1979) pp.303–45.

When he first wrote about this, Poulantzas rather disarmingly remarked that there was no theoretical homogeneity between these two notions;[11] but he later took pains to explain that structures and class practices are not 'ontologically distinct domains'. The point of distinguishing them is to show that 'social classes, although objectively determined (structures), are not ontological and nominalist entities, but only exist within and through the class struggle (practices)'.[12] So while class practices cover 'the entire range of the social division of labour' we can nevertheless separate 'structural class determination' from 'class position in a given conjuncture'. The first of these categories – structural class determination – which is the principal defining characteristic of classes, fixes both their place in the division of labour, and also their interests. But classes sometimes take up 'class positions' which are out of line with these interests – they form alliances with classes whose interests are antagonistic to their own, adopt strategies doomed to defeat, and so on – and the second of Poulantzas' categories is designed to accommodate this pheno-menon. It does not contribute to the *definition* of a class – for he is adamant that the *class positions* adopted by particular groups are not indicative of their true class membership. As he puts it:

The labour aristocracy...in certain conjunctures takes up class positions that are in fact bourgeois. This does not mean, however, that it becomes, in such cases, a part of the bourgeoisie; it remains, from the fact of its structural class determination, part of the working class, and constitutes, as Lenin put it, a 'stratum' of the latter. In other words, its class determination is not reducible to its class position.[13]

While this distinction is obviously important to Poulantzas, it is not immediately clear that it helps him to unite structures and class practices as he intends. In fact, it appears merely to strengthen the divide between them, by defining structural determination in terms of structures and class position in terms of practice. However, Poulantzas is emphatic that the two are interconnected, and his claim seems to be founded on a further belief about class position. To return to the case of the labour aristocracy, even when its position is out of line with its structural determination, 'this structural determination...is necessarily reflected in working-class

11 PP and SC, p.68.
12 'Reply to Miliband and Laclau', *New Left Review* 95 (1976) p.82.
13 C in CC, p.15.

practices ('class instinct' as Lenin used to say) – practices that can always be discerned beneath its bourgeois "discourse", etc'.[14] So while there may be a superficial disparity between the structural determination and the position of a class, the latter will always be responsive to the former at some level, and it will always be possible to discern the role of class determination in the class struggle.

The starting point of Poulantzas' theory is thus a view of capitalist society as a bipartite whole, made up of contradictory structures and class practices. It now remains to ask what role is played by the state in this totality, and Poulantzas' initial reply is quite straightforward. The state acts as a mediator, aiming to reconcile the contradictory forces and interests of the society so that it is able to function and reproduce itself. Furthermore, because the state fulfils this function, the contradictions of the formation are 'condensed' in its own structure, so that it can be used as a sort of map of society at large.

Even at this stage, we can see an indication of this function of the state in the fact that, although it is a factor of cohesion in the formation's unity, it is also the structure in which the contradictions of the various levels of a formation are *condensed*. It is therefore the place in which we find reflected the index of dominance and overdetermination which characterises a formation or one of its stages or phases. The state is also the place in which we can *decipher* the unity and articulation of a formation's structures.[15]

According to this view, the state is a doubly important object of study, first because its institutions are a major and influential part of the political instance of capitalist society, and second because they are the key to the working of society as a whole. Poulantzas therefore develops his theory by elaborating his conception of the capitalist state and tracing its connection with the class struggle. So far, the state has been characterised as a structure – as part of the political instance, integrated into the whole structured in dominance. However, Poulantzas argues that, in smoothing over the structural contradictions of society and rendering it coherent, the state simultaneously maintains existing classes. In 'constituting the factor of cohesion between the levels of a social formation', it 'maintains in the ensemble of structures, that place and role

[14] 'Reply to Miliband and Laclau', p.82.   [15] PP and SC, p.45.

which have the *effect* (in their unity) of dividing a formation into classes and producing political class domination'.[16] The task of the state apparatuses is therefore to mediate between the conflicting interests of classes. But in doing this they do not wield a power which is independent of the class struggle. Rather,

State apparatuses...materialise and concentrate class relations, relations which are precisely what is embraced by the concept 'power'. The state is not an 'entity' with an intrinsic instrumental essence, but is itself a relation, more precisely the condensation of a class relation.[17]

In order to see what this involves, it is helpful to look closely at Poulantzas' account of classes. Most important of all, he thinks of them as determined by political and ideological as well as economic factors from which they derive political, ideological and economic interests. In some cases these interests match up, so that a course of events which realises a class's economic interests will simultaneously realise its political and ideological ones as well. But more often a class will achieve an economic interest at the expense of an ideological one, or an ideological one at some cost to its political strength, and this interplay of interests in the course of the class struggle contributes to an exceedingly complex class structure. Classes are divided into 'strata' and 'fractions', are forever making and breaking alliances, and are analysed now in terms of their structural determination, now in terms of their position in the conjuncture. Poulantzas thus constructs what appears at first to be a morass of categories in continual flux; but he then extracts from it a pattern of relations which he regards as constant. In any social formation there is at least one class which, by virtue of its various determinations, is dominant in the sense that it is better placed to realise its interests than its rivals. Sometimes a single class may dominate at all levels, economic, political and ideological. But in a more complex formation there might, for example, be a politically dominant class and a distinct economically dominated class, each divided into strata and fractions with interests which to some extent diverge.

Now, the stability of a social formation can only be maintained if no class with any means of imposing its interest is pushed to the point of revolt. If the profit margins of manufacturers are too drastically reduced they may move their capital from the industrial

[16] PP and SC, pp.44, 51.   [17] C in CC, p.26.

to the financial sector; if the political power of the unions is legislated against they may make their power felt at the economic level by going on strike, or at the political level by withdrawing from established parliamentary parties – and so on. If the state is to prevent the class struggle from destroying an existing set of structures it must be in a position to further class interests which are not too damaging to the formation as a whole, and to prevent classes from realising interests which would have gravely divisive consequences. To achieve this, Poulantzas says, it must to some extent be independent of *all* classes, or as he puts it, it must be relatively autonomous. The capitalist state is thus to be seen as an autonomous set of institutions, able to intervene at all levels in order to maintain the *status quo*.

While the state has to have *some* autonomy to fulfil its role, it is by no means completely independent. It is true that it must be able to check the excesses of even the ruling class; but Poulantzas also has to account for the tendency of capitalist states to favour capitalist interests. His explanation begins by assuming that, as a matter of definition, dominant classes are well placed to put pressure on the institutions of the state, so that the interesting question is why they should ever put up with having their interests thwarted. The first part of his answer appeals to the class struggle. One might think that a politically dominant class would be able to impose its interests on a formation as a whole and take control of the state. This, however, is rarely feasible because such a class is generally too fraction-ridden to 'realise its political unity on the basis of a politically conceived common interest'. Only a force which stands outside the manoeuvring and hostility of the struggle can hope to make any headway in furthering a particular interest.

Poulantzas next distinguishes between the economic and political interests of the dominant classes. The state, he claims, may sometimes fly in the face of the short-term *economic* interests of this class; but it will not damage their political interests, and in this way political order is maintained.

The capitalist state characterised by hegemonic class leadership, does not *directly* represent the dominant classes' economic interests, but their *political interests*: it is the dominant classes' political power centre, as the organising agent of their political struggle.[18]

[18] PP and SC, p.190.

As it stands, this claim raises more problems than it solves. Why, one immediately wants to ask, can the state be relied upon to foster the political interests of the dominant class? Why should the other classes in the formation put up with it? And why does the dominant class submit to leaving some of its economic interests thwarted so long as its political interests are satisfied? In replying, Poulantzas ritually warns that these matters depend to some degree on the particular conjuncture – the extent to which the state can act autonomously varies with the balance of power within the class struggle. But he also justifies his account in general terms. Capitalist modes of production, he says, are marked by a curious paradox. Their conditions of work bring people together more than ever before, in factories, offices and towns; and yet at the same time these people are isolated from one another. As producers they are separated from their means of production; the law treats them as possessors of free will and responsibility, and the impression is strengthened by the dominant ideology.

This isolation, which is an over-determined but real effect, is experienced by the agents according to the mode of their competition; it ends by concealing from these agents the fact that their relations are class relations. This isolation applies just as much to the capitalists/private owners as to the wage labourers, although it clearly does not appear in the same way in the socio-economic relations of these two classes.[19]

The members of society thus perceive themselves as private individuals, each pursuing their own private and competing interests. In the midst of this free-for-all, the state appears as the guardian of the *common* interest, a force able to check rapacious greed, protect the weak and defenceless and uphold the values of the polity; in short, a set of institutions which, though not neutral, are not allied with any one class.

This account of the state as it is portrayed by the dominant ideology of capitalist societies is held to explain why the dominant and the dominated classes both tend to put up with it. They perceive it as standing for the interest of society as a whole, and are constrained by this ideological view to tolerate its infringements of their sectarian interests, providing that these are not too severe. Of course, for the dominant class this does not require so much patience: its political interests are satisfied, as is the spirit – if not

[19] PP and SC, p.275.

the letter – of its economic ones. The dominated classes need more ideological bolstering. But where this is successful, they will link their fortunes to capitalism, and will not even see the state as an oppressive part of the class struggle.

Poulantzas' explanation gives a key role to the relation between the capitalist state and capitalist ideology. But it remains to ask again why the state's policy of pursuing the common interest always fosters the political interest of the ruling class. Why do the two always coincide? Why does Poulantzas believe that the autonomy of capitalist states is always subject to this limit? As usual, he is emphatic that the answer has nothing to do with the individuals who actually run the state. Senior bureaucrats, it is true, are sometimes members of the dominant class, and sympathise with its aims. But this does not explain the state's overall function; for even when it is controlled by officials drawn from other classes, it continues to serve the political interest of the hegemonic fraction. To get at the true explanation we must concentrate on the fact that the bureaucracy's 'particular functioning is *not directly determined by its class membership*, by the political functioning of those classes and functions from which it originates: it depends on the concrete functioning of the state apparatus, i.e. on the place of the state in the ensemble of a formation and on its complex relations with the various classes and fractions'.[20] However, while this tells us how *not* to solve the problem, it is less clear what positive steps we are to take – a dilemma to which I shall return later in the chapter.

Although this brief outline cannot do justice to the complexity and detail of Poulantzas' work, it does convey enough of its character and aspirations to form the basis of a critical discussion, and in this part of the chapter I shall focus on three connected questions, all concerned with the explanatory power of the theory. The first and most obvious point concerns the wide range of categories Poulantzas posits in order to capture the workings of capitalist formations. Are these sufficiently closely defined for us to be able to apply them to particular cases? The second question makes the same sort of enquiry about the relations between categories. Are we able to test claims, for example, about the way the state mediates between classes in a particular conjuncture? Poulantzas

[20] PP and SC, p.335.

himself is content to rely on counterfactual arguments in support of certain relations, but I shall suggest that these are less conclusive than he supposes. Finally, it is important to ask whether his account of the class struggle avoids voluntarism as he claims it does. For if his theory is to succeed in overcoming the evasions which mar Althusser's work, his critics must be satisfied on all these three heads.

My discussion of the first two questions will revolve around Poulantzas' notion of 'pertinent effects'. This concept has been much haggled over, and it may seem both unfair to Poulantzas and unrevealing of his work as a whole to pick on its Achilles' heel. But although it is an easy target, its deficiencies are exhibited quite generally, if less glaringly, throughout the theory. And it has the advantage of enabling us to consider the two problems associated with terms and relations in a single context.

Among the most striking features of Poulantzas' theory is the huge number of categories it posits in order to explain one aspect of capitalist society. A formation, for instance, is a whole structured in dominance made up of various instances, each of which contains structures. Among the effect of these are classes, subdivided into strata and fractions, some dominant, some subordinate, some hegemonal, all with practices, and with interests, economic, political and ideological. The interplay of these terms is not always easy to grasp, but the point of positing them is comparatively clear. For Poulantzas wishes to achieve two goals. On the one hand his account must be sufficiently unified to provide simple, powerful explanations of the state and its role in the class struggle. On the other hand it must be subtle and flexible enough to accommodate the diverse forms of capitalist society, and to be immune to refutation by counter example. Poulantzas responds to this second requirement with what Laclau has aptly called 'taxonomic fury', and in doing so runs the risk of defeating his other goal.[21] For as he increases the number of categories in terms of which phenomena are to be explained, he at the same time multiplies the number of relations between them; and since each factor is in some way dependent on a large number of others, the resulting range of possible variations is immense. This certainly makes room for the many capitalist configurations found in history. But some of

---

[21] Ernesto Laclau, 'The Specificity of the Political' in *Politics and Ideology in Marxist Theory* (London, 1977) p.70.

Poulantzas' critics have complained that, instead of creating a theory, all he has provided is an overblown list – a set of descriptive categories so various as to be applicable to any social formation, and lacking any explanatory bite.

The area of the theory to which this criticism seems most obviously to apply, and the context in which it has been most discussed, is Poulantzas' account of the defining characteristics of classes. As we have already seen, classes are defined in the light of a variety of factors, political and ideological, as well as economic, so that, as he puts it:

A class can be considered as a distinct and autonomous class, as a social force, inside a social formation, only when its connection with the relations of production, its economic existence, is reflected on the other levels by a specific presence.[22]

But this only raises another question: how do we know a specific presence when we see one? Poulantzas' answer is best introduced in his own words.

It can be said that this presence exists when the relation to the relations of production, the place in the process of production, is reflected on the other levels by *pertinent effects*. These 'pertinent effects' can be located in political and ideological structures as well as in social, political and ideological class relations. We shall designate by 'pertinent effects' the fact that the reflection of the place in the process of production on the other levels constitutes a *new element* which cannot be inserted in the typical framework which these levels would present without this element. This element thus transforms the *limits* of the levels of structures or of class struggle at which it is reflected by 'pertinent effects'; and it cannot be inserted in a simple variation of these limits.[23]

The concept of 'pertinent effects' is then used in the definition of several sub-groups of classes. First there are *strata* – groups that can 'without being social forces, exert an influence on the political practice of these forces'. Then there are *autonomous fractions* 'which constitute the substratum of eventual social forces'. Finally there are *fractions* – 'ensembles which are capable of becoming autonomous fractions, according to the criterion of pertinent effects'.[24]

The fact that the definitions of these terms are extremely murky can in part be traced to the notion of pertinent effects. How do we know, critics have asked, what effects are pertinent? Surely

[22] PP and SC, p.78.   [23] PP and SC, pp.78–9.   [24] PP and SC, p.84.

Poulantzas is simply relying on the intuitions of social theorists, assuming that they will be able to discern a set of connections that he is unable or unwilling to spell out?[25] Poulantzas' reply to this criticism is instructive, partly because it tells us more about pertinent effects themselves, but also because it casts light on his general approach. He agrees, first of all, that he has not provided an account of the precise character of pertinent effects, but argues that it would be a mistake to do so. It would be useless to lay down in advance what they are, since they vary with each particular state of affairs.

It is clear that the characteristics of 'pertinent effects' and of their novelty relative to the typical form of the levels always depend on the concrete conjuncture of a concrete historical situation. It is only by examining this that we can circumscribe the relations of the limits and variations, and thus characterise the 'pertinent effects'. This pertinence may be reflected in important modifications of political and ideological structures as well as in modification of the field of the political and ideological class struggle.[26]

To some extent, then, Poulantzas concedes his critics' point. As he says, 'My text requires a certain sensitivity to the political problems of the class struggle on the part of the reader, since it is entirely determined by the theoretico-political conjuncture'.[27] But he does not regard the charge as a serious objection to his theory. In this, however, he may be naive, for unless he is prepared to say what pertinent effects are, it is not clear what grounds he has for claiming that they always exist. And this immediately raises a further difficulty.

It is clear that Poulantzas originally posited the idea of a pertinent effect in order to save a particular claim of Marxism. His objective

was to attack directly those conceptions according to which the working class has become either integrated or dissolved in contemporary capitalism ...My aim was to show that even when the working class has no revolutionary political organisation and ideology...it still continues to exist as an autonomous and distinct class, since even in this case its 'existence' has pertinent effects on the politico-ideological plane. What

[25] R. Miliband, 'Poulantzas and the Capitalist State', *New Left Review* 82 (1973) p.86; E. Laclau, *Politics and Ideology in Marxist Theory*, p.71.
[26] PP and SC, p.81.
[27] 'Reply to Miliband and Laclau', p.68.

effects? Well we know that social democracy and reformism have often amounted to quite considerable ones.... [28]

This passage helps us to understand the dilemma Poulantzas is trying to solve. In order to avoid the pitfalls of economism he has argued that classes are defined at all levels, not just at the economic one. But in some capitalist societies the working class seems to have no distinct political organisation or ideology, and so appears to lack any defining characteristics at these levels. To offer purely economic criteria for its identity would be to slide back into economism. And to argue, as some theorists have done, that the class has dissolved or been integrated into the bourgeoisie would be to abandon the hope of a proletarian revolution heralding the end of capitalism. Poulantzas therefore takes a third way out: he claims that, despite superficial appearances, the economic position and practice of the working class *does* have 'pertinent effects' at the political and ideological levels, so that it can be identified as a class after all.

The difficulty with this is that theory and observation are unbalanced. As often in Poulantzas' work, the motive for a particular claim is a theoretical one, and the world is forced to fit it. Given his definition of class, Poulantzas has got to find traces of the working class in the political and ideological spheres. But since this is sometimes exceedingly difficult, he would be unwise to say exactly what sort of traces they should be; for he would then be vulnerable to the criticism that in some capitalist formations these are simply not to be found. By positing the vague conception of 'pertinent effects' Poulantzas overcomes this particular problem. But it is still not clear why there must always be such effects in social formations, other than because their absence would upset one solution to a dilemma posed by Marxist theory.

The problem, then, is why one should accept Poulantzas' claim that pertinent effects are a constant feature of capitalist social formations. And it might seem that it would at least be a start to discover whether they are in fact common. But this brings us back to our original question: how do we identify them? The vagueness of Poulantzas' definition, and his motive for positing the term at all combine to produce a considerable gap between theory and explanation which is by no means confined to this case.

[28] 'Reply to Miliband and Laclau', p.69.

Although Poulantzas does not give a direct answer to the question 'How are we to know a pertinent effect when we encounter one?', he does discuss an historical example which may throw light on the matter. To demonstrate his criteria for class identity he chooses the case of the French peasantry during the eighteenth Brumaire, and asks whether or not they were a class. As is well known, Marx himself gave a somewhat ambiguous answer; but Poulantzas' reply is quite clear.

They constitute precisely a distinct class to the extent that their place in the process of production is reflected in this concrete conjuncture, at the level of political structures, by the historical phenomenon of Bonapartism which would not have existed without the small peasant farmers... (T)he economic existence of the small-holding peasants is reflected, on the political level, by the 'pertinent effects', constituted by *the particular form of state* of Bonapartism as a historical phenomenon.[29]

Furthermore, we can imagine a hypothetical case 'where the economic existence of the small-holding peasants is not reflected by Bonapartism.'

In this case, of course, their particular place in the process of production is anyway manifested by a certain presence at the political level, if only in the simple fact that the political organisation of the other classes, as well as the institutions of the state, have to take into account the existence of the small-holding peasants...However, in this case, this presence neither constitutes a 'new element', nor has 'pertinent effects', but is only inserted as a variation into limits circumscribed by the pertinent effects of other elements, for example into the framework of constitutional democracy. It is clear in this case that the small-holding peasants do not constitute *a distinct class.*[30]

In this discussion, Poulantzas relies on a counterfactual claim to defend his view that the peasantry had a pertinent effect at the political level – namely Bonapartism – and were thus a distinct class. If they had not exercised precisely the sort of power which is the distinguishing mark of a class, Bonapartism would never have arisen.

This sort of argument is so commonly used in the social sciences that it almost passes unnoticed; but as soon as one stops to think about it one is faced with the problem in hand. How does Poulantzas know that the counterfactual claim he proposes is true? On what ground does he conclude that the form of the Bonapartist state is an effect of the small-holding peasantry, rather than of some other factor or factors? On what grounds, therefore, does he identify Bonapartism as a pertinent effect? The general function of the state as an instrument of social cohesion presumably justifies the assumption that its form will be tailored to an existing set of structures and class practices. But why, in this case, should it 'reflect' the existence of the peasantry in particular?

Although the analysis of counterfactuals is both difficult and contentious, they are generally used in the context of a certain sort of theory.[31] If they are to have any explanatory bite it must first be possible to pick out particular causal connections against a fairly stable set of background conditions. Some phenomena may simply not lend themselves to this kind of analysis. Sometimes, for example, a factor which is identified as the causal antecedent of an effect may be so interlinked with numerous other conditions that, while it is true that if that factor had not been present the effect would not have existed either, it is hardly illuminating. For had the causal factor not been present, everything would have been different. Some of Poulantzas' own claims seem prone to this sort of problem: the hegemonal position of a class, for instance, is a function of its economic, political and ideological roles, of the form of the state, of its relations with other classes and functions, and the state of the class struggle. The fact that it *is* hegemonal of course has numerous effects. But to say of a particular consequence that it would not obtain *if* that class were not hegemonal does not tell us much. Since another class presumably *would* then be hegemonal, all class relations would be changed, the state would be different, the dominant ideology would be different, and so on. An instructive counterfactual must, therefore, pick out two causally connected events or states of affairs which are relatively independent of other factors. And to do this at all one obviously needs a general account of the relation between them.

Unfortunately, Poulantzas' example does not satisfy the first of these requirements. We are told that 'the economic existence of

---

[31] For a general discussion of the role of counterfactual analysis in the social sciences see J. Elster, *Logic and Society* (New York, 1978) ch.vi and S. Lukes 'Elster on Counterfactuals', *Inquiry* 23 (1980) pp.145–55.

the small-holding peasants is reflected, on the political level, by the "pertinent effects" constituted by the particular form of state of Bonapartism'. And we are also told that there could be a case where the peasantry had no such effect. But we are not told what features of the French peasantry are to be held responsible for Bonapartism, nor what features of Bonapartism are attributable to the French peasantry. Neither does Poulantzas explain what the peasantry would have been like if it had not had this pertinent effect, except in so far as he stipulates that they would not then have been a class. Here, the explanatory power of the assertion is reduced by the fact that a relation is said to hold between two very general terms – the peasantry and the state. And because they are so general, the complementary counterfactual claims are unilluminating.

So much for the terms of Poulantzas' theory. If we now consider the relations he posits between them we find ourselves facing a comparable problem; although he posits numerous interconnections between the components of social formations, he neither explains how he arrives at them nor describes them in any detail. In part this is due to a desire to avoid a rigidly causal account which will straitjacket capitalist societies into a single position, not allowing for their diversity and variation. For example, although the Bonapartist state is a pertinent *effect* of the peasant class, this is not meant to imply that there is a unidirectional causal link between the peasantry and Bonapartism. Rather, Poulantzas says, 'What makes them function concretely as a distinct class, as a social force, is in fact the historical phenomenon of Bonapartism',[32] thus seeming to imply that the two are interconnected in such a way that each can only exist in conjunction with the other. The relations Poulantzas appeals to, such as contradiction, determination or reflection, are therefore in a way deliberately vague, and intended to capture what Althusser calls 'structural causality'. But while there may be degrees of determination or contradiction, there must be some consensus as to what count as examples of these relations – what sorts of contradiction are there? How do things determine one another? – and Poulantzas himself intensifies the difficulty by using these terms in an alarmingly general fashion. Contradictions, for example, are said to plague the relations of classes, of structures, and even of individuals, as in '[The big

[32] PP and SC, p.80.

employers in France] have sought a policy of compromise towards
the working class, in the context of their own contradictions with
banking monopoly capital and non-monopoly capital – witness
the contradictions between Giscard d'Estaing and Chaban-
Delmas.'[33] Some of his well-wishers have pointed out that it is
difficult to *use* relations as general as these to provide more than
schematic explanations, and have attempted to define them more
precisely. Erik Olin Wright, for example, has broken down the
concept of 'determination' into six distinct relations: structural
limitation, selection, reproduction/non-reproduction, limits of
functional compatibility, transformation and mediation.[34] These
are still very general in the sense that they tell you what *kind* of
relations you would have to look for to turn Poulantzas' scheme
into an explanatory tool, rather than what relations of these types
there actually are. For example, structural limitation 'constitutes
a pattern of determination in which some social structure establishes limits within which some other structure or process can
vary, and establishes probabilities for the specific structures or
processes that are possible within those limits'.[35] And, even
relations such as these may not be enough to back up counterfactual
claims like the one Poulantzas offers. For they are presented as
holding between structures, or between a structure and the class
struggle, and it is so far only an article of faith to suppose that
they can be refined to a point where one can identify a specific
connection such as that between an aspect of the peasant class and
a particular form of capitalist state.

Starting from Poulantzas' counterfactual example, I have suggested that the categories and relations he discusses are, as they
stand, too abstract to provide any grounds for such claims, and
indeed are too schematic to yield detailed explanations of particular
historical events. But the argument might as well be put the other
way round: his inability to formulate counterfactuals is just one
consequence of the difficulties attendant upon a theory of such
scope and grandiloquent abstraction. Yet Poulantzas' wish to
argue hypothetically is peculiarly revealing; for as well as drawing
attention to the slight explanatory power of his theory it raises the
third of the questions with which I began – the question of

---

[33] C in CC, p.155.
[34] Erik Olin Wright, *Class, Crisis and the State* (London, 1978) pp.15–26.
[35] *Ibid.*, pp.15–16.

whether he has really succeeded in casting off voluntarism. This issue is crucial to an assessment of thoroughgoing holism such as that developed by Althusser, and therefore deserves careful attention.

Theorists who reflect about the ways in which things might have been different are bound to consider the question of what might have *made* events take another course. One class of variables – avalanches, sudden heart attacks, meteorites and so on – which can be loosely classed as natural disasters, are comparatively unpredictable and unlikely. No doubt half the population of Paris could have been wiped out by a typhoid epidemic in 1788, and perhaps the king would not then have been sent to the guillotine. But speculations of this sort are founded on such improbable premises that they do not help us to understand what actually happened, and merely prompt the rejoinder, 'So what?' The art of counterfactual analysis consists in formulating *probable* hypothetical claims which will help us to disentangle the roles played by disparate variables, and this requires a systematic view of the kinds of factors which might plausibly have been different. Those social scientists who regard human actions as undetermined will look to them as the basis of counterfactual claims. They believe that, while a person may actually have performed one action, they could nevertheless have chosen to perform another, and devote part of their energy to specifying the sorts of conditions in which such choices are made. But this approach, which elevates individuals into subjects, is of course not available to Poulantzas. He can blithely agree that, in other circumstances, individuals would have acted differently. But he must go on to explain the sorts of variations which have this effect on individuals (or other subjects) if he is to rely on counterfactual claims about the actions of subjects. To justify his view that there are ways in which things might have been different while at the same time avoiding voluntarism, Poulantzas argues that there are two sources of valid counterfactuals. The first is the structures of a society. A division of labour, for example, might have been different in ways that would have affected the system of education. But while this suggestion is plausible enough, it raises the question whether the shapes of structures are to be explained simply in terms of one another, the political responding to the ideological, the ideological to the economic, and so on. Poulantzas claims that they are not and introduces, as a second source of variation, the class struggle. In order to understand the history of capitalist societies one must look not just to their structures, but also to the balance of power between classes *and the way this power is exercised.* What actually happens depends to some extent on the strategies that classes pursue and on the unity with which they organise themselves and seize opportunities to strengthen their positions. For instance, if the working class parties of pre-fascist Germany had really represented the class itself, the latter would have been more easily aroused than it in fact was, and the rise of fascism would at least have been a greater struggle.

Poulantzas must therefore take into account both social structures and the class struggle to understand the course of events. As he says:

The nature of the relations between the state and the field of the class struggle belongs to the type of relations which hold between the structures and this field. The capitalist state, in which the specific autonomy of instances is located by its relation to the relations of production, *sets the limits* which circumscribe the relation of the field of the class struggle to its own regional structures. In other words, these state structures, as they appear in the relation of the instances, *carry inscribed within them a set of variations* which in delimiting the class struggle achieve concrete reality according to the effects which this struggle has on the state within the limits thus set. Henceforth, when we say that in a capitalist formation certain characteristics of the class struggle are related to the capitalist state, it must not be understood as meaning that these characteristics are a simple phenomenon derived from its structures or that they are exhaustively determined by them. It must be understood as meaning that the field of the class struggle has fundamental effects on this state, effects that are realised within the limits set by its structure to the extent that they control a set of variations.[36]

However, it remains to be seen how the class struggle, and the part it plays in history, are to be analysed. In particular, can Poulantzas explain specific conjunctures and the shifting relations between classes without tacitly relying on some sort of voluntarism? He, of course, does not admit any difficulty of this kind, but I shall suggest that his appeals to class strategy are treacherous, and reintroduce the conception of subjects that he is so anxious to stamp out. This brings us to the third, and for our purposes

[36] PP and SC, pp.187–8.

the most significant, of the problems laid out at the start of this section.

Scattered throughout Poulantzas' studies of the phases of capitalism are appeals to the strategies adopted by classes in order to realise their interests.[37] At first glance these appear anachronistic, for our ordinary understanding of the term 'strategy' embodies the idea of intentional action. If a class is to lay plans there must be a strategist who assesses the circumstances, evaluates possible outcomes and decides what to do; and while these properties can be attributed to groups as well as individuals, an agent (what Poulantzas would call a subject) is needed in both cases. Strategy, in this everyday sense, is incompatible with the abolition of the subject, and it is therefore reasonable to suppose that Poulantzas is not proposing to explain the course of the class struggle in terms of the ingenuity exercised by classes and class members in realising their goals. But to avoid this return to voluntarism he must have in mind some further conception of strategy, and it is not surprising to find him talking about it in what might be called its objective sense: the strategy of a class – the course of action which will best enable it to gain power over other classes – is estimated in the light of its objective interests and its position in a formation, and is detached from the beliefs and aspirations of its members. In discussing the rise of fascism in Germany, for example, Poulantzas claims that, 'With the end of the First World War, a genuinely revolutionary period opened in Germany and Italy. Revolution was on the agenda, in the sense that there were conjunctures of objectively revolutionary situations. But the working class failed to take State power...and to secure its objectives in critical situations.'[38] He then goes on:

It is certain that in [Germany and Italy] there was at least a significant failure by the working class to achieve the political objectives imposed by and attainable in a situation of open crisis. For a working-class defeat is not simply to be measured in terms of its failure to take State power, to 'make the revolution', a possibility which did not exist or no longer existed in the two cases mentioned; it can also be measured in terms of its inability, in an open crisis, to attain 'possible' political objectives, falling short of the seizure of state power, as part of a long-term strategy.[39]

[37] This problem is also evident in 'Towards a Democratic Socialism', *New Left Review* 109 (1978) pp.75–87.
[38] *Fascism and Dictatorship*. trans. Judith White (London, 1974), p.139. Hereafter abbreviated to F and D.   [39] F and D, p.140.

Hence the strategy of the working class is worked out in terms of the opportunities open to it in a particular situation – or rather in terms of the opportunities that Poulantzas claims *would* have been open to it had the class itself been quite different. But strategy of this sort, while it is a useful analytic tool, does not contribute much to historical explanation. For we still have to understand what makes the difference between situations where classes pursue their objective interests and situations where they stray from them.

Perhaps the most obvious course is to elucidate the strategies of classes by appealing to the constraints under which they labour. Given its position in the struggle and the structures of a capitalist formation, a class may not be left with many options. And as long as its strategy conforms to one or some of these, the task of explanation is relatively well defined. Among the explanations given by Poulantzas which fit this pattern, his account of the transition from non-monopoly to monopoly capital is a case in point. He begins by reminding us that monopolies have not progressively wiped out non-monopolies, as the traditional Marxist model predicts, but have tended to reach agreements with them instead. This is sometimes taken to show that the process of monopolisation has come to a halt. But Poulantzas argues that this interpretation is a mistake because the policy actually serves the interests of monopolies better than any available alternative, and is thus in line with their strategy.

In considering the history of the relationship between monopoly and non-monopoly capital in the Imperialist metropolises, it appears that, confronted by the struggle of the popular masses and the resistance of non-monopoly capital, monopoly capital has been led to a selective strategy involving indirect forms of subordination of non-monopoly capital, so that it can avoid serious fissures in the power bloc...Current forms of dependence are...distinct from the 'wild' forms of liquidation and takeover of non-monopoly capital that were particularly characteristic of the first phase of monopoly capitalism...These changes in strategy, of which anti-trust legislation in the United States was only one aspect, must be interpreted as concessions by monopoly capital to non-monopoly capital within the power bloc itself...The main significance of these strategic compromises must be understood...What they essentially effect is the rhythm (acceleration and deceleration) and forms...of the concentration process...They are positive in the context of the balance of forces, in the sense that the effects of the concentration process are not as negative for non-monopoly capital as they would have been without these compromises.[40]

In this case, the 'strategic compromises' of monopoly capital are said to be imposed by the balance of power between classes in the power bloc – a balance which might itself be explicable in structural terms. But although explanations of this kind provide some understanding of the class struggle, it is clear that Poulantzas does not regard them as enough. In the first place, they presuppose that classes correctly perceive the constraints of their situations and modify their strategies accordingly, and Poulantzas elsewhere acknowledges that it would be extremely rash to make such an assumption. Discussing revolutionary situations, for instance, he remarks a trifle sadly that 'unless the revolutionary organisations have a conscious and adequate strategy', which they frequently lack, opportunities for change will go unnoticed. So the actual behaviour of classes must be taken into account. Secondly, explanations of strategy that appeal only to external constraints do not allow for the possibility that a class may have a range of interests, not all of which can be satisfied by any single policy. As an example of this problem Poulantzas cites the negotiations which resulted in the French Sixth Plan. It would have suited the economic interests of monopoly capital if the plan had proposed a high rate of growth. But its political interests would have been – and were – better served by a lower growth-rate; for this was less damaging to non-monopoly capital and the working class, and therefore did not provoke such hostility to monopoly capital. Poulantzas comments that

What should not be forgotten here is that we are dealing with a political balance of forces within the bourgeoisie itself, in the context of its confrontation with the working class. The forms and tempo of the concentration process...are often simply strategic measures that serve the political interests of monopoly capital by ensuring its political hegemony over the bourgeoisie as a whole... The long period of French 'backwardness' (in the process of concentration) cannot be entirely explained by the 'structural economic' weakness of French capitalism... The weakness was related to the particular type of compromise that French monopoly capital was forced to make with non-monopoly capital...for political reasons related to the struggle of the working class.[41]

[40] C in CC, p.144.   [41] C in CC, pp.145–6.

Faced with this dilemma, monopoly capital puts its political interests above its short-term economic goals, and compromises with the other sections of the bourgeoisie. But it remains to ask if Poulantzas can explain this 'choice', 'policy-decision', or 'process' without treating classes, or even their members, as subjects.

Holistic explanations such as those employed by Althusser and Poulantzas are peculiarly prone to the charge of incompleteness. We can learn an enormous amount from studying the constraints imposed upon classes, whether by structures or the class struggle, but they cannot resolve all the questions we wish to ask. In trying to bridge the gap, theorists commonly resort to purposive forms of explanation, and Poulantzas' appeal to class strategy is an apt example of this phenomenon. Strategies are usually made by strategists. But if voluntarism is to be avoided, the tactics followed by classes, their members or representatives cannot be explained in terms of the qualities of either individuals or groups. What they are capable of in the way of understanding and manipulating their own situation is itself determined by the whole structured in dominance, and the idea of strategy itself must be understood in holist terms. Poulantzas recognises this, but is unable to put the principle to work. For in his analyses of the classes of capitalism he resorts to purposive terminology, without giving any hint of how this is to be understood except in an everyday, voluntarist manner. Many examples could be given, of which I shall mention two. First, German National Socialism is said to have

handled its main enemy, the working class, and the latter's reaction to other popular classes, *by a calculated plan to divide it.*[42]

[My italics]

Secondly, Poulantzas denies that the falling rate of profit characteristic of capitalism is an inevitable feature of the mode of production. Rather, the continuing tendency to a falling rate of profit

depends on the class struggle: it is well known that the tendency for a falling rate of profit is always combined with a tendency for a rising rate of surplus value. This 'countervailing' effect itself depends on the cost of reproduction of the labour force, and so on the rate of exploitation. The question which then arises is... up to what point, in what determinate

[42] F and D, p.193.

conjuncture, and by what means can the dominant class exploit the dominated classes – *i.e. in what way and how will the latter in the end allow themselves to be exploited* on both the national and international levels.[43]

[My italics]

In the first of these passages National Socialism has 'a calculated plan'. But calculation, in the ordinary sense, requires individuals to assess, judge, choose and decide. In the next passage Poulantzas argues that the course of capitalism partly depends on what the working class 'allows'. Yet our everyday understanding of this term is intimately connected with the idea of choice. By drawing attention to these links I have no wish to insist on the virtues of 'ordinary language' analysis. Instead, I hope to show that Poulantzas relies, for the explanatory force of these claims, on our pre-theoretical, voluntarist understanding of them, and thus fails to provide us with examples of the holistic form of explanation he advocates. Each of the two passages raises rather different problems, and together they will enable us to connect the issues of counterfactual analysis and voluntarism which have so far been treated separately.

The claim that a class may or may not allow itself to be exploited is another case of Poulantzas' belief that the course of the class struggle is not altogether determined by the structural constraints of a particular phase of capitalism. A hegemonal class may be more or less ingenious at furthering its political interest while maintaining its position in the power bloc; the working class may make better or worse use of a revolutionary situation. However, Poulantzas would presumably argue that in any given case the course of events is determined by antecedent factors. In Germany just after the First World War, for example, working class organisations were so far removed from both the objective interests of the class and the concern of its members that they were incapable of seizing the revolutionary opportunities open to them. The point of counterfactuals, on this view, is not to suggest that at any particular moment something else might have happened, but to indicate and test the relations between causes and consequences.

The belief that any particular event is determined, although the course of events as a whole is not, is problematic in itself. But if

---

[43] F and D, p.41.

that is put on one side we are brought back to the question of
what kinds of determining factors Poulantzas invokes in order to
explain what actually happens. Sometimes, as we have seen, these
include the strategies adopted by classes – for instance, National
Socialism's calculated plan to divide the working class. And since
we are familiar with Poulantzas' rejection of voluntarism, we shall
assume that this in turn is to be explained in a way that avoids
treating either individuals or classes as subjects. The choices,
assessments and selections which go into formulating a strategy,
and the ingenuity or crassness displayed in implementing it, must
themselves be shown to be determined by factors other than
intentions.

This, though, is where Poulantzas lets his readers down. For
instead of taking the final explanatory step, he leaves them with
an unanalysed notion of class strategy. They know how *not* to
analyse it, it is true, but are given no positive guidance which will
enable them to get around the menace of voluntarism. If we now
ask how we are able to get any grasp of the explanatory role of
class strategy in Poulantzas' theory, the answer is that we rely on
our everyday, voluntarist understanding of it. We use this to cast
light on a metaphor of which we are given no other interpretation.
But this, of course, does not yield explanations of class strategies,
and thus of the class struggle, which are in line with Poulantzas'
theoretical principles. And the assumption that they can be given
is grounded on faith alone.

VI

◇ ══════════════════════════════════════ ◇

Concessive holism and interests: the *Annales* school

The claims of absolute holism explored in the two preceding chapters are clearly both interesting and provocative, and have given rise to a series of fertile debates within the social sciences. It remains true, however, that we do not now have the means to deploy this approach wholeheartedly, so that anyone who insists on its universal applicability must be taken, at least for the moment, to be committing an act of faith. Whatever understanding of societies we gain in future, we do not *now* have a theory of ideology capable of explaining the myriad ways in which individuals perceive their situations, nor a theory of the social determination of character that will account for the vicissitudes of history. As a result, theories of the type proposed by Althusser and Poulantzas cannot honour their own claims to completeness. The kinds of difficulties that we encountered in Poulantzas' work continually crop up, and the tacit use of counterfactuals which rely on individualist premises is a perennial stumbling block.

These difficulties are sometimes tolled as the deathknell of holism and the victory of individualism. However, the problem can by no means be so readily dismissed. As we have seen, the divide between individualism and holism is too deep for the inadequacy of one approach to provide an automatic vindication of the other; and more important, holism is not so easily killed off. The recognition that we cannot give complete holist explanations of social phenomena does not undermine the centrality of the intuition to which the doctrine, in its various forms, is a response: the sense that many properties of individuals, whether tastes, aspirations, beliefs, expectations or habits, are to an overwhelming extent formed by society. The question of how we are to construct explanations that reflect this insight is not swept away by the conclusion that one approach to the task is inadequate, and the problem therefore remains as pressing as ever.

In a further attempt to come to terms with it, a number of social theorists have concentrated on exactly the sort of counterfactual analysis that we found used, but not discussed, by Poulantzas. By asking what conditions would have obtained if particular individuals had behaved differently, they have aimed to give a clearer analysis both of the defining characteristics of holism, and of its relations to individualism. As a result, they have arrived at a view which I shall call 'concessive' holism. Exponents of this approach aim to overcome the deficiencies of absolute holism by sacrificing its claim to completeness, and their concession therefore consists in abandoning the Althusserean dogma that there is just one mode in which to explain *all* social phenomena. They insist, nevertheless, on the distinctiveness and importance of holism, and, as I shall argue, their account suggests a way to resolve the dispute between holists and individualists.

The central problem with which holism has to deal – the problem that gives rise to the holist view I shall now examine – can be very simply expressed. Social scientists aim to understand a course of events which is shaped by a diverse range of factors – by trade markets, the supply of raw materials, education, the bombs thrown by terrorists, government policies, and many other things. It sometimes seems that individuals have a startling impact on this pattern which can only be understood by appealing to specific psychological traits. Napoleon's military victories, for example, might just have to be attributed to his genius; Britain's adherence to a monetarist economic policy throughout 1981 might in the end rest on Margaret Thatcher's supreme obstinacy. But we do not know how to account for these characteristics as the results of antecedent social factors, and, indeed, have very little idea what circumstances, if any, produce military genius or obstinacy. So it seems that, to legitimate our appeal to such traits, we must allow an element of individualism to enter social explanations. We must allow that the course of events is partly to be explained by appealing to individual characteristics.

Among social theorists who have attempted to defuse this type of individualist threat, two principal lines of argument have been followed out. The first is based squarely on the suggestion that it is simply an illusion to suppose that any truth, or any significant role in social explanation need be assigned to counterfactuals of

the form, 'If individual X had not had the psychological
characteristic a, they could not have performed action b and event
p would not have occurred.' Such statements are in fact usually
false, either because the combination of a and b is not a necessary
condition of p, so that even if X had not done b, p might still have
occurred, or because, even if X hadn't done b, some other agent
would have done it instead, thereby bringing about p. This view,
if it could be adequately defended, would successfully stave off
individualism by denying it a significant part in social explanation;
but to establish the point is far from easy. A representative and
influential attempt was made by Plekhanov in his essay, *The Role
of the Individual in History*,[1] where he considers what effect the
characters of prominent people such as kings and statesmen have
on the course of events. He then goes on to ask the same question
about people with extraordinary talents, whether in physics,
generalship or painting.

In the first part of his argument, Plekhanov allows that the
psychological characteristics of individual actors can influence the
course of historical events. Powerful actors, especially, are able
to make a difference to things; for example King Louis XV's
lasciviousness made him indulgent toward Madame de Pompa-
dour, who was therefore able to protect the position of the
incompetent General Soubise in spite of the fact that his army was
unreliable in defending France's military interests. Had Louis been
less concerned with sex, Plekhanov suggests, France might well
have fared differently during the Seven Years War. However, the
causal influence of such characteristics cannot be considered by
itself, and must be investigated in the context of particular
societies. For

The possibility of exercising this influence, and its extent, are determined
by the form of organisation of society, by the relation of forces within
it. The character of an individual is a 'factor' in social development only
where, when, and to the extent that social relations permit it to be
such.[2]

So far so good. Plekhanov next goes on to claim that the character
traits of individuals, whether causally efficacious or not, are

[1] George V. Plekhanov, 'The Role of the Individual in History' in J. Allen
ed. *Fundamental Problems of Marxism* (London, 1969).
[2] *Ibid.*, p.102.

'accidents' in relation to 'the historical destiny of nations'.[3] To keep to the same example,

Louis XV's lasciviousness was an inevitable consequence of the state of his physical constitution, but in relation to the general course of France's development the state of his constitution was *accidental.* Nevertheless, as we have said, it did influence the fate of France and served as one of the causes which determined this fate.[4]

Here, the psychological characteristics of individuals, the outcome of a person's childhood experiences and physical constitution, are contrasted with some other range of causal factors responsible for 'the course of France's development'. And in labelling the former causes 'accidents', Plekhanov implies that they are both an unpredictable and a comparatively unimportant part of the explanation of the course of historical events. The question of the essay – What effect do individual actors have on the course of history? – is thus partly answered by the very terms in which it is posed. For we are told at the start that the effects of their psychological traits are 'accidents', as opposed to the main stuff of social explanation.

Having slipped in this normative bias, Plekhanov goes on to consider whether a series of accidents might not change the course of history. Could an unusual concatenation of talents and characters, placed in a situation where they were able to exercise their influence, upset the destiny of nations? He concludes that they could not, on the basis of two connected arguments. He first claims that accidents are unable to outweigh 'social needs', which can be traced to the social relations of a society, themselves ultimately caused by its productive forces. For example,

The urgent social need of France at the time of the 18th century was the substitution for the obsolete political institutions of new political institutions that would conform more to her economic system. The most prominent and useful public men of that time were those who were more capable than others of helping to satisfy this most urgent need.

We will assume that Mirabeau... [was a man] of that type. What would have happened had premature death not removed [him] from the political stage? The constitutional monarchist party would have retained its considerable power for a longer period; its resistance to the republicans would, therefore, have been more energetic. But that is all. No Mirabeau

could, at that time, have averted the triumph of the republicans.
Mirabeau's power rested entirely on the sympathy and confidence of the
people; but the people wanted a republic, as the court irritated them by
its obstinate defence of the old order. As soon as the people had become
convinced that Mirabeau did not sympathise with their republican
stirrings they would have ceased to sympathise with him; and then the
great orator would have lost nearly all influence, and in all probability
would have fallen a victim to the very movement that he vainly would
have tried to check.[5]

In this passage Plekhanov makes the straightforward claim that,
while individuals can hasten or hold up the course of events,
determined by the 'social needs' of a society, generated by its
forces of production, they cannot change it. He does not, however,
explain *why* the causal influence of the forces of production is
always, and necessarily, greater than that of individuals, and only
takes up this point in a second argument, in which he shifts from
the discussion of character traits to consider the role played by
individuals of extraordinary talent. Talents, he says, are themselves
the product of social relations, and only appear when social
conditions allow.

It has long been observed that great talents appear whenever the social
conditions favourable to their development exist. This means that every
man of talent who *actually appears*, every man of talent who becomes a
social force, is the product of *social relations*. Since this is the case, it is clear
why talented people, as we have said, can change only individual features
of events, but not their general trend; *they are themselves the product of this
trend*; were it not for that trend they never would have crossed the
threshold that divides the potential from the real.[6]

These arguments contain an embarrassing number of suppressed
premises, invalid inferences and equivocations. For our purposes,
however, their most serious fault is Plekhanov's *assumption* of the
truth of a thoroughgoing holism, which wreaks havoc with his
reasoning. Central to his argument is the claim that the course of
events is principally to be explained in terms of the social needs
of a society, needs which ultimately rest upon the forces of
production. 'Accidents', while they have effects on political, social
and economic life, cannot divert the trend of history. To defend
this view one has to explain why the causal power of individuals
is thus limited. Why is it that 'accidents' of personality or talent

can never outweigh the influence of the forces of production and social relations? Why is their effect always short-lived and superficial? In his two arguments, one dealing with accidents of personality, the other with individuals of exceptional talents, Plekhanov addresses these questions. But his answers are far from satisfactory. The first argument simply asserts that social factors outweigh individual ones. And the weakness of this claim is compounded by his examples, which are far more individualist than the claim they are intended to illustrate. The fate of Mirabeau, for instance, would have been sealed by the lack of *sympathy* felt for him by the people, on account of their *irritation* with the Court's defence of the old order. Here psychological traits are invoked to account for the inability of psychological traits to alter the progress of history, a confusion of which Plekhanov seems unaware. But leaving this muddle on one side, the main difficulty is the complete lack of any defence of the conclusion.

The second argument is a little fuller, but no better. The talents of individuals, it suggests, are themselves the outcome of, and are explained by, various aspects of the social environment. (Thus where talents are concerned a determinist story can be told.) However, as we saw in Chapter v, this view is difficult to sustain, and certainly should not be asserted in so cavalier a fashion. In his discussion of accidents of personality Plekhanov offers *no* defence of his claim that these can never outweigh the causal influence of the mode of production and resulting social relations. And in his discussion of the parts played by people of exceptional talent he simply asserts that these individual capacities are to be explained as the result of social circumstances. *What* circumstances he does not say. But in any case, the truth of this determinist claim is exactly what would have to be proved in order to substantiate Plekhanov's thesis.

If holist forms of explanation are to merit serious consideration, they must clearly be based on more than an uncritical acceptance of a crude version of historical materialism, and the claim that they are not threatened by counterfactuals such as those discussed at the start of the chapter must be given a less doctrinaire justification. Underlying Plekhanov's argument is the central idea that, in order to explain a social phenomenon, one must understand not just why it did (or does) in fact occur, but why it would have happened even in the absence of the particular beliefs and actions that caused it. The imposition of this 'necessity constraint' on holist explanation is enough to separate it from the individualist view that to describe the individual traits which caused a social phenomenon *is* to explain it. However, if this holist conception is to provide a standard for at least some explanations within the social sciences, and if it is to avoid the difficulties discussed in Part II, it is obvious that it will need to be greatly refined and elaborated.

Contemporary social theory, however, does not lack for attempts at elaboration. One of the most interesting has recently been proposed by Richard Miller,[7] who elaborates his claim by means of an example – the identification by capitalists of the bourgeois and national interests.

Marxists and many other people believe that the following large-scale social phenomenon is characteristic of modern societies: a typical, major, active capitalist regards the interest of big business as coinciding with the interests of the nation as a whole. In other words, he believes that actions and policies which maximise, on the whole, the wealth and power of the large firms which dominate his nation's economy also maximise, on the whole, the welfare of the people of the nation...

It might be felt that a typical capitalist identifies the bourgeois and the national interests as a result of his encounters with evidence indicating that this identity holds. The belief in question could then be explained individualistically, as due to the businessman's reasons for forming the belief, namely, his possession of other, evidential beliefs and his desire to form an accurate notion of the national interest on the basis of the evidence available to him. If Marxists are right, however, in their conception of the activities of the bourgeoisie, this explanation is not typically true. Especially in advanced capitalist societies... major, active capitalists are seen as strike-breakers, war-makers and instigators of periodic political repression, who are in possession of overwhelming evidence to the effect that the bourgeois interest and the interest of most people in the nation are not identical.[8]

This disparity between the evidence available to major capitalists and the beliefs they hold suggests, according to Miller, that their beliefs are to be explained in the following way:

A typical major capitalist identifies the bourgeois and the national interest because such a belief serves a variety of his desires and goals. For

[7] Richard Miller, 'Methodological Individualism and Social Explanation', *Philosophy of Science* 45 (1978) pp.387–414.
[8] *Ibid.*, pp.397–8.

one thing, he has a goal of promoting this belief in others. And it is easier and less tense to encourage a belief in others if you share it. Also, he possesses overwhelming evidence that policies of lay-off, speed up, pollution and war which he instigates or encourages hurt most people. If he were to accept this conclusion he would feel much the worse for it. So, to achieve the peace of mind he desires, he must encounter the evidence strongly prejudiced toward the belief that the interests of big business actually coincide with the interests of most people, despite apparent evidence to the contrary. Of course, these desires and goals are not *his* reasons for making the crucial identification. He would emphatically, honestly and severely reject this explanation of his belief.[9]

Some people will want to quarrel with this analysis; but for our present purposes its accuracy is less important than the use Miller makes of it. For he distinguishes sharply between two questions. We might ask, first of all, 'Why do the particular people who are major capitalists, namely, John D. Rockefeller III, David Lindsay, Walter Wriston, and others, typically identify the bourgeois and national interests?'[10] And the answer to this may be given in terms of the individual histories of these men. But if the spirit of the Marxist analysis is correct, we need to know the answer to a second question, 'Why, in a modern capitalist society, would major capitalists, whoever they might be, typically identify the bourgeois and national interests, even if Rockefeller, Lindsay and the other actual capitalists were to have different life histories?'[11] And the answer to this is not to be found in the histories of individuals.

The individualist causes of the fact that a capitalist typically identifies the bourgeois interest and the national interest may include this father's saying this to his son, who will become a capitalist, this company president's congratulating the second vice-president for this speech, and so on. But if the father had not said anything like that...if the president had not said anything like that...the schools, media and less formal training-processes of our society would...ensure that others who became capitalists generally identify the bourgeois and the national interests.[12]

Miller's argument therefore hinges on a counterfactual claim. He asks whether a general phenomenon would cease to be a feature of a society if particular individuals held different beliefs. And he concludes that, since it would not, the individual beliefs cannot be the explanation of the general phenomenon.

[9] *Ibid.*, p.398.   [10] *Ibid.*, p.404.   [11] *Ibid.*   [12] *Ibid.*, p.411.

While the example Miller discusses conforms to the type of explanation advocated by Althusser, the two theorists nevertheless defend very different positions. For Althusser, as we saw, all explanations of social phenomena must be holistic. Miller, by contrast, holds that holist explanations are appropriate whenever a specific condition is met – whenever a social phenomenon would persist if the relevant properties of particular individual members of a society were different. His argument is therefore compatible with the view that there may be cases where this does not obtain, which require to be explained in individualist terms. However, Miller goes on to cast doubt on the status of such individualist explanations when he suggests that holist explanations are the stuff of social science, whereas individualist ones are something else. In Chapter II we found that a good deal of social science has been informed by this view; but it is nevertheless natural to wonder why individualism should be excluded from the group of disciplines that aim to provide us with a grasp of the social world. Why should we not derive from them an understanding which includes a knowledge of both the individual causes of particular social phenomena and the holistic forces underlying them? In fact, if the social sciences are really to explain the social world, would it not be wiser to retreat from the demand that they must conform to a single standard of explanation, and allow instead that they may encompass a variety of projects?

Miller himself argues for his view that the distinction between holist and individualist explanations marks the boundary between science and non-science by claiming that it is an established feature of social scientific practice. This seems questionable; the lack of consensus within the social sciences as to what sort of explanations they can and should provide rather suggests that both holism and individualism are fiercely adhered to.[13] However, it is interesting and important to consider whether there might be a theoretical justification for Miller's view, relatively independent of the present habits of social scientists: a reason for holding that social scientific explanations *should* satisfy a necessity constraint of the kind Miller describes. For this would obviously ensure pride of place for holist explanations. Unfortunately, perhaps, it is hard to see how Miller's demand that the social sciences should deal *only* in holist explanations can be reconciled with his (and our) account

[13] See, for example, the debates discussed in Chapter III.

of the difference between holism and individualism. This difference, as we have seen, is between two kinds of causal explanation, and if both can have some force, as Miller believes, it is not obvious why social scientists should restrict themselves to only one of them.

Despite his desire to secure the dominance of holism by equating it with social scientific explanation, Miller's argument only sustains a weaker claim; for his distinction between holism and individualism suggests that there is a place for both types of explanation. This may seem an innocuous conclusion. In fact, however, it marks a major transition in the terms of the debate, and separates the concessive form of holism sharply from the absolute form considered earlier. As we saw, absolute holists are opposed to the very idea of individualist explanations; they defend the supremacy of their own view, which they regard as incompatible with individualism. Concessive holists, by contrast, look on individualism with more favour. Aware that absolute holists cannot live up to their own tenets, they offer a different distinction between the two approaches so that, rather than being seen as strict alternatives, they are held to be complementary. Instead of the question, 'Which form of explanation is right?', concessive holists ask when holist and individualist explanations are appropriate. They therefore allow that some phenomena may be elucidated in individualist terms, while at the same time claiming a major place for holist explanations.

If the problem is interpreted in this way, the debate between holists and individualists centres initially on the relative scope of the two approaches. How much can be explained in individualist terms, and how much in holist ones? But it is an implication of concessive holism that there will be no hard and fast answer to this question; the reply will depend on our ability to establish the relevant counterfactuals, which will presumably change with our theories about the social world. At first glance, therefore, concessive holists appear to take a purely pragmatic view of the relations between holism and individualism. However, the matter cannot be left there. If concessive holists are to provide a *solution* to the problem of holism rather than a mere rule of thumb, they must justify their claim that holist and individualist explanations are, if not complementary, at least capable of coexistence. As we saw in Chapter III, much of the longstanding disagreement between exponents of the two views stem from their commitment to distinct and incompatible conceptions of the individual (a commitment which gives rise, on one side, to absolute holism). Concessive holists cannot simply ignore this divide, as Miller does, for this will leave their own position undefended. They are therefore faced with the task of overcoming it. How might one reconcile the two approaches, while yet acknowledging the deep-rooted differences between them?

The beginning of an answer to this question is implicit in the accounts of concessive holism we have so far considered. For these suggest that holism and individualism can fruitfully be seen as serving different *interests* in social explanation.[14] Holists, according to Miller, aim to show why social phenomena would be as they are even if particular individuals possessed properties other than those they actually have. And the explanations they offer go back to the social wholes which form and constrain individual people. In a quite different vein, individualists who look to the properties of individuals to explain social affairs are inspired by a belief in a conception of autonomy. Another way to express this motivating power of individualism is to say that we have a tremendously strong interest in explaining at least some social phenomena in individualist terms, since this enables us to explain ourselves to ourselves; to see what it feels like to be in someone else's shoes. As autonomous actors we create and modify the social world, bringing about events and states of affairs which would not otherwise have occurred. To explain a social phenomenon is therefore to capture its uniqueness and show why it happened when it need not have done.

These two projects – on the one hand a wish to investigate the constraining influence of social wholes, and on the other a desire to understand the shaping power of individuals – answer to different sorts of concern with the social world. To regard these as distinct *interests*, each of which sustains a set of values, allows us to reformulate the question of the relative scope of holist and

[14] The suggestion that the social sciences answer to diverse explanatory interests tends to be explored only tentatively. For some provocative and relevant speculations see B. van Fraassen, *The Scientific Image* (Oxford, 1980) pp.97–157; H. Putnam, *Meaning and the Moral Sciences* (London, 1978); R. Rorty, 'Method, Social Science and Social Hope' in *Consequences of Pragmatism* (Minneapolis, 1982); Barry Barnes, *Interests and the Growth of Knowledge* (London, 1977); J. Habermas, *Knowledge and Human Interests*, trans. J. Shapiro (Boston, 1971).

individualist theories which we found to be such a pressing one. For instead of aiming to divide the available explananda between two types of explanation, allocating some to holism and others to individualism, the extent to which either is applicable can be seen as relative to our interest in understanding the social scene. To gain a fuller grasp of the strength and scope of concessive holism and of individualism we must ask what interests they serve and what kinds of enquiries they satisfy. Only a richer conception of what they are trying to provide will enable us to make a sensitive assessment of their achievements and potential.

An appreciation of the interests which underlie holist and individualist modes of explanation cannot be gained by thought alone. Just as a desire to understand absolute holism led us to analyse the substantive claims of Althusser and Poulantzas, so we must now consider work inspired by an attachment to concessive holism in order to reach a clearer view of its guiding interests. Among those whose practice can be shown to conform to this approach, there can I think be no doubt that the most important, in contemporary social science, have been the historians of the *Annales* school.[15] Their impact has of course been immense. As a fellow historian sums it up,

No group of scholars has had a greater impact, or a more fertilising effect, on the study of history in this century than the French historians of 'the *Annales* school' – that is, to speak in more concrete terms, the historians whose base is the 6th Section of the École Practique des Hautes Études in Paris... and whose regular organ is that ample and ever-expanding periodical originally entitled *Annales d'histoire économique et sociale* and now – that is, since 1942 – *Annales: économies, sociétés, civilisations*. French in origin, French in inspiration, these historians now form an international élite, held together by a distinct philosophy and a corporate loyalty.[16]

For the purposes of my present argument, however, of even greater importance than the influence exercised by *Les Annales* is

[15] See P. Burke, 'Reflections on the Historical Revolution in France: The Annales School and British Social History', *Review* 1 (1978) pp.147–56; T. Stoianovich, *French Historical Method: The Annales Paradigm* (Ithaca, 1976); P. Hutton, 'The History of Mentalities: The New Map of Cultural History', *History and Theory* 20 (1981) pp.237–59; Robert Forster, 'The Achievements of the Annales School', *Journal of Economic History* 38 (1978) pp.58–76.
[16] H. Trevor Roper, 'Fernand Braudel, the *Annales* and the Mediterranean', *Journal of Modern History* 44 (1972) p.468.

the fact that their approach is clearly governed by the idea –
definitive of concessive holism – that individualist and holist
explanations are best seen as answering to different interests, and
therefore as contributing, at least to some extent, to independent
projects. It is to the *Annales* school, and more particularly to the
assumptions governing their work, that I therefore turn, aiming
to show how they have successfully applied the precepts of
concessive holism to a wide range of subject, and in this way to
suggest how the idea that holist explanations answer to a certain
interest can be developed and defended.

   While it would be misleading to present the members of the
Annales school as a wholly homogeneous group committed to a
single methodology, they nevertheless hold in common a number
of views about the study of the past. Their work can be seen as
a range of attempts to deal with a shared set of problems which
have perhaps been most clearly formulated by the greatest among
them – by Bloch and Febvre (the founders of the journal) in the
first generation, by Braudel in the second, and more recently by
Le Roy Ladurie. In discussing the school I will draw on the work
of the last two writers, who focus particularly clearly on the
theoretical issue with which we are concerned.

   The crusading spirit of the early members of *Annales* derived
in part from their opposition to the way history was practised. In
the first place, diplomatic and political history were regarded as the
centre of the discipline – the transaction of government business
from month to month and year to year so that, according to the
progenitors of the new approach, one could be forgiven for
thinking that the only Frenchmen who had lived were cabinet
ministers. But even worse than this neglect of anything that
happened outside the courts of Europe was the way that political
history was distilled into a narrative, based on whatever literary
evidence was at hand. For not only was history of this sort
anecdotal, prey to the prejudice and impressions recorded in
diaries, letters or dispatches that happened to have survived. It was
also unduly limited in the kind of explanations it offered of the
course of events, explanations which appealed overmuch to the
actions and dispositions of individuals, stringing them together
into a complex story of aims and intrigues. In Braudel's words,
it was a 'refuge des passions et des jugements gratuits, domaine

du descriptif'.[17] If history was to become a respectable discipline, according to the contributors to *Annales*, it would have to eschew both this form and content. Instead of an anecdotal narrative it must aspire to the rigorous standards of a science. The narrow confines of political life must give way to *total* history, offering rich explanations of the multifarious aspects of the past.

These two aspirations are closely linked. 'L'histoire totale' is, for the members of *Annales*, in part the history of all sorts and conditions of men and women: of merchants and artisans, peasants and beggars, nurses and midwives, as well as ministers and aristocrats. But it is also a history which tries to take account of the whole range of factors that shape human societies, from the character of their physical environments to sporadic peasant rebellions. Rather than selecting the particular class of political events as the stuff of history, and then seeking to explain it by appealing to the play of national and personal interest, the *Annales* school advocates eclectic research into such diverse topics as economics, populations, social institutions, technologies and climate, designed to contribute to a complete picture of social life. This demand for a broader perspective trenches on the form and content of history in that it involves both enquiry into new areas and novel modes of explanation. However, because of their desire to promote the idea of history as a scientific discipline, the *Annales* school have not been equally well disposed to all aspects of the past. Their opposition to political history stemmed in part, as we have seen, from their hostility to impressionistic narratives, and in their anxiety to escape this they have tended to favour subjects susceptible to quantitative analysis. Thus much of their reputation is based on the results of statistical surveys of climate, demographic trends, price curves, and other quantitative indicators of growth and decline.

In defending this choice of subject matter Le Roy Ladurie has recently protested that it represents just whatever can be most readily understood in quantitative terms. The study of politics, and ideas in general, which has so far lagged behind, must ultimately be incorporated into total history, and will become more accessible as the techniques of quantitative history grow in sophistication.

[17] F. Braudel, 'Pour ou contre une politicologie scientifique', *Annales: économies, sociétés, civilisations* 18 (1963) p.119.

But that this is not the whole explanation can be seen from the fact that the members of *Annales* do not treat 'l'histoire totale' as a homogeneous body of facts and theories which all fit neatly together like a vast jigsaw. Rather, they rely on a tripartite classification, originally set out by Braudel, to divide it into three distinct elements.[18]

Braudel's categories are based on the idea that it is possible to distinguish various historical 'times'.[19] Of course, the past constitutes a single 'time' in the sense that events can be arranged in chronological order. But within this complete chronology we can discern some processes and states of affairs that are comparatively brief, others that last for an intermediate length of time, and some that go on for centuries or even millennia. Within the first class of *événements*, for example, are the brief spans of individual lives; within the second are economic trends and cycles lasting several generations; and in the third, the *longue durée*, are factors such as population size which may remain unchanged over long periods.

The choice of duration as the organising category of the past may seem arbitrary, or at best superficial; but Braudel implies that it serves to pick out states and processes of qualitatively distinct types, which have different sorts of impact on human affairs and demand to be studied separately. In *La Méditerranée* he describes these three 'histories'. First comes the *longue durée*, 'in which all change is slow, a history of constant repetition, ever-recurring cycles'.[20] Next comes the level of *conjonctures*, 'of groups, collective destinies and general trends', which must 'meet two contradictory purposes. It is concerned with social structures, that is with mechanisms that withstand the march of time; it is also concerned with the development of those structures. It combines, therefore, what have come to be known as *structure and conjoncture*, the permanent and the ephemeral, the slow moving and the fast.'[21] Finally there are *événements*, 'surface disturbances, crests of foam that the tides of history carry on their strong backs. The history

[18] F. Braudel, 'History and the Social Sciences' in P. Burke, ed. *Economy and Society in Early Modern Europe* (London, 1972) pp. 11–42.
[19] For an interesting discussion see J. Hall, 'The Time of History and the History of Times', *History and Theory* 19 (1980) pp.113–31.
[20] F. Braudel, *The Mediterranean and the Mediterranean World in the Age of Philip II* 2 vols., trans. Sian Reynolds (London, 1972) p.20.
[21] *Ibid.*, p.236.

of brief, rapid, nervous fluctuations, by definition ultra-sensitive; the least tremor sets all its antennae quivering.'[22] Total history must take account of all these – hence the organisation of *La Méditerranée*, which is divided into three parts. But the historians of *Annales* have usually shown a preference for the history of the *longue durée* and of *conjonctures*, and Braudel, in particular, is hostile to the study of mere *événements*. To understand the reasons for this choice, and to appreciate the work it has yielded, one must consider these fundamental categories more carefully.

At first glance it appears that Braudel has merely hit on a convenient fashion of dividing up the past, to bring it under control and make it easier for historians to encompass. It goes without saying that a huge range of factors play some part in shaping the course of human affairs, and there are obvious advantages in a division of labour. However, while this is true, it misses the point; for Braudel's choice of categories is guided by more than pragmatic considerations, and is based on a view of historical explanations. The phenomena of the *longue durée* are background conditions that help to explain *conjonctures*, which in turn contribute to the explanation of *événements*. 'Resounding events are often only momentary outbursts, surface manifestations of these large movements *and explicable only in terms of them*' [my italics].[23] But what does each of these categories contain, and how are they related?

The idea of the *longue durée*, as it was originally formulated was quite straightforward. Human life is affected and constrained by material factors that are comparatively permanent. The climate partially determines what crops can be grown, the quality of the soil partially determines their yield, the size of a population partially determines the area of land it can cultivate, and so on. Thus a detailed knowledge of the material conditions in which communities have lived will tell us about the constraints under which they have laboured; and this in turn will help us to understand some of their properties.[24] Such basic considerations, however, tend to provide more information about what was impossible than about what occurred, and their explanatory power is therefore limited. We may know, for example, that vines cannot

[22] *Ibid.*, p.21.   [23] *Ibid.*
[24] See, for example, Le Roy Ladurie, *Times of Feast, Times of Famine*, trans. Barbara Bray (London, 1972).

be grown in areas where the average annual temperature is lower than 52°F, and can thus infer that they could never have been grown in Edinburgh. But even if we discover that vineyards vanished from south east England at a time when the climate was getting colder, we still do not know for sure why they disappeared. Perhaps it was because of the weather. But the change might equally well be due to economic factors which made vine growing unprofitable. The study of the purely material aspects of the *longue durée*, while fascinating in itself, and in some ways theoretically undemanding, is therefore only capable of telling us a little of what we want to know. Perhaps it is for this reason that, in Braudel's work at least, it is much more generously defined to include various stable but non-material factors. The trade routes of the Mediterranean, for example, and the volume of traffic they carried, help to explain the location, size and wealth of towns, which in turn affect their character as centres of commerce or industrial production.[25] Such features 'become stable elements for an indefinite number of generations'.[26] Or, a more surprising inclusion, 'examples of permanence and survival are to be found in the immense domain of culture': the Latin civilisation of the late Empire, the 'outillage mentale' of the sixteenth century outlined by Febvre, or the geometrical treatment of pictorial space.[27]

Additions such as these certainly enrich the idea of the *longue durée*; but at the same time they complicate it by broadening the notion of constraint on which it depends and obscuring its relationship with *conjonctures*. As we saw, geographical conditions are of interest to historians because they put constraints on society. The same can no doubt be said of any 'outillage mentale'. But the relevant sense of constraint, and the aspects of society that are constrained in the two cases, are vastly different; and if the *longue durée* is to be more than a ragbag of everything that endures these disparities would have to be elucidated. An awareness of these pitfalls has encouraged Braudel's successors to use the notion of the *longue durée* in a comparatively narrow sense to designate stable features of the environment which can be seen to constrain social *conjonctures*.

Moving on to consider the category of *conjonctures*, we find

---

[25] Braudel, *The Mediterranean* pp.282, 319.   [26] *Ibid.*, p.18.
[27] Braudel, 'History and the Social Sciences', pp.18–19.

problems parallel to those we have discussed occurring in, if anything, an exacerbated form. The first is the question of its scope. *Conjonctures* were originally viewed, it seems, as structures and processes of intermediate duration. Unlike their counterparts in the *longue durée*, they were seen not so much as steady *constraints* with which societies had to contend over long periods, but as patterns of change which were themselves part and parcel of social life. Thus among the most frequently cited examples of *conjonctures* are the increase in the population of western Europe during the sixteenth century, the rise and fall of European prices from 1791 to 1817 and 1817 to 1832, and the pattern of wages during the same period. Apart from the fact that they can be measured, movements such as these are interesting because they can be used to explain other *conjonctures*, particularly changes in social structure. The size and character of Mediterranean towns, for instance, responded to population growth, as did the size of land-holdings among the swelling ranks of the peasantry. Because social changes which can be fitted into comparatively lengthy processes are yoked together with some structures in a single category, much of the history of *conjonctures* consists in relating one to another. And this enterprise has proved extremely fruitful.

There remains, however, an interesting problem of definition. In the case of processes, the division between those that make up the *longue durée* and those that belong to the sphere of *conjonctures* is bound to be rough; there is no absolute division between a gradual increase in population lasting for a century and a cycle of growth and decline lasting a mere seventy-five years, a fact reflected in the organisation of *La Méditerranée*.[28] And the same can be said of *structures*. In practice, the distinction between the two categories seems to reflect, as I have suggested, the existence of two kinds of interest in the past: on the one hand a concern with steady constraints on social life, and on the other an interest in large-scale patterns of change. But the relevant changes are further defined by being unintended and at least to some extent beyond the control of the societies they affected, either because of their intrinsic character, or because of the scale on which they occurred. The increase in the size of the European population during the sixteenth century provides a particularly striking example of such a transition, for while it can be fairly accurately

[28] Braudel, *The Mediterranean* pp.326–8, 394–415.

charted and measured, its causes are not well understood. We do not really know why a greater number of people began to survive into adulthood during this period. Nevertheless, the fact that there was such a change casts light on a number of other *conjonctures* which permanently altered the character of European society. Le Roy Ladurie argues, for example, that the pattern of land-holdings in the south west of France was affected – they were increasingly divided up among the members of expanding families, so that the income of peasants fell. On a broader geographical scale, the level of food production ceased to be enough to feed everyone, so that famine became an endemic problem, and institutionalised ways of dealing with vagrants and paupers began to be established throughout Europe. Also on an international scale, the price of grain rose in response to demand, and this in turn affected wages.[29]

History of this sort, which offers to explain the relations between properties of societies, has been enormously successful in the past thirty years or so and provides a clear conception of how the underlying interest of holism can guide social enquiry. We may be more anxious to understand the *constraints* on individual actions and intentions, as well as the various kinds of factors that bypass them altogether, than the actions and intentions themselves. However, in order to discover whether the history of the *longue durée*, and of *structures* and *conjonctures*, can be couched in the strongly counterfactual form spelled out, for example, by Miller, and can thus qualify as an example of concessive holist explanation, we need to consider its relations to the actions and intentions of individuals much more carefully. The *Annales* school attempts to deal with this issue by appealing to the third category identified by Braudel – that of *événements*; but to say quite what *événements* are is no easy task. Braudel himself seems to think of them as brief episodes without significant consequences. 'Personally, I should like to imprison [the term] and restrict it to the short-term. The event is explosive, it is something new...It blinds the eyes of contemporaries with clouds of smoke; but it does not endure, and its flame is hardly visible.'[30] This definition is marked by an evasion which runs through all Braudel's work: first, *événements* are brief; but in addition, they 'do not endure', they are surface

---

[29] Le Roy Ladurie, *The Peasants of Languedoc*, trans. John Day (Chicago, 1974) pp.73–83.
[30] F. Braudel, 'History and the Social Sciences' p.14.

manifestations of...larger movements.'[31] The implication that
they are determined by other factors and of slight consequence
occurs again and again; but Braudel can never bring himself to
say it straight out, and indeed undercuts it in the third part of *La
Méditerranée* where, for example, the defeat of Charles V and the
Venetians by the Turks in 1538 is said to have had consequences
which lasted over a third of a century.[32]

This vacillation arises, in part, from the fact that such a variety
of phenomena are classed as *événements*. Wars, battles, the
processes culminating in the breakdown of alliances, individual
judgments, decisions and actions are all included, and the various
tools of the traditional political historian are used to explain them.
Individuals, by the force of their personalities, are held responsible
for the breaking of truces: 'It was thanks to [the Pope] at any
rate, that [the truce] was broken. That one man should have
revived, alone and with such speed, a still smouldering war, gives
one to reflect on the role of individuals in the dramatic episodes
of history' (sic).[33] Imperial policies are explained by individual
passion and affection. 'And yet this man [Charles V] was still
possessed by one passionate desire: to pass on to his son Philip,
the inheritance intact. It was a dream dictated both by politics and
by affection, for he loved this orderly, thoughtful and respectful
son, the disciple he had schooled himself, both personally and
from a distance.'[34] Similarly, a Spanish defeat by the French is put
down to Charles V's stubbornness;[35] the lackadaisical course of
the war with the Turks is attributed to the Spanish lack of funds;[36]
and so with many other examples.

The catchall character of this category undoubtedly makes it
more difficult for the members of the *Annales* to develop any clear
sense of its relation to the history of *structures* and *conjonctures*. Yet,
if the central issues of both the nature and scope of holist
explanation are to be investigated further, it is vital that such
connections should be unravelled. If we want to know when the
counterfactuals definitive of holist explanation can be sustained,
we shall have to study the links between constraints such as those
imposed by the *longue durée* and the attributes of individuals in
considerable detail; and this in turn requires the separation of the
latter from the *mélange* of *événements*. The failure to come to terms

[31] F. Braudel, *The Mediterranean* p.21.   [32] *Ibid.*, p.906.   [33] *Ibid.*, p.938.
[34] *Ibid.*, p.914.   [35] *Ibid.*, p.925.   [36] *Ibid.*, p.932.

with this task casts light on, though it does not excuse, the hectic character of the final part of Braudel's *Méditerranée*: even when connections are traced between *conjonctures* and the actions of individuals, they tend to leave the actions heavily under-determined – so much so, in some cases, that they are barely explained at all.

It remains true, nevertheless, that if the members of the school wish, as they say they do, to write 'total history', they must perforce deal with the relations between the properties of social wholes and those of individuals, which are the main focus of concessive holism. This problem is most explicitly addressed by Le Roy Ladurie, and I shall reconstruct his view from his study *The Peasants of Languedoc*.

The opening chapters of this book trace the economic and demographic forces that shaped rural life in Languedoc throughout the fifteenth and sixteenth centuries: the steady growth of the population, its effect on landholdings, the agriculture of the region, the deterioriation of real wages, and so on. The central section, 'New States of Consciousness and Social Change' then deals with a range of beliefs and attitudes which are said to have followed in the wake of these developments, and in particular with what Le Roy Ladurie calls 'a deep and sometimes lasting permutation in peasant mentality'.[37] The most dramatic outward sign of this change, according to Le Roy Ladurie, was a series of peasant rebellions which occurred at intervals throughout the sixteenth and seventeenth centuries. Whereas country life had before been relatively quiescent, it now became unsettled and the foci of dissatisfaction altered; protests against taxes were regularly staged from about 1540, and after 1550 gave way to larger-scale insurrections such as those at Romans in 1580, in the south west during the 1590s, and, much later, the Camisard rebellion in the Cévennes which began in 1688. Le Roy Ladurie's explanation of this transition invokes, first of all, the rapid spread of the French language to the land of the *langue d'oc* during the sixteenth century. Because this diffusion was not even, and was far more marked where levels of literacy were comparatively high, it resulted in the growth of two cultural zones: on the one hand, French-speaking regions receptive to 'foreign' ideas, and on the other, rural areas

[37] Ladurie, *The Peasants of Languedoc* p.149.

which retained the old language and the old ways of life. This change paved the way for Protestantism, which first took hold where French was spoken – in a number of towns, and in the socially atypical mountains of the Cévennes – and then spread to other rural areas. The opposition to the Catholic church fostered by Calvinism was thus one important cause of anti-tithe strikes. But it coincided, as Le Roy Ladurie is quick to point out, with the economic interests of the peasantry, whose standard of living was steadily declining.

Economic and religious factors are therefore held to play important and complementary parts in the explanation of peasant unrest: for those who lived off the land, conditions were grim and unyielding, and Calvinism offered a way of life which might, among other things, free them from the burden of the tithe. However, Le Roy Ladurie sees the strikes and uprisings of this period as expressions of frustration rather than campaigns for political change. In his view the peasantry (and indeed society as a whole) was caught in a conceptual bind; for although Protestantism provided the rudiments of a revolutionary ideology, it also distracted attention from the economic and political conditions which were the real source of their plight.[38] Intellectually unequipped to understand their position in society, peasants were correspondingly unable to see how to transform it, and their protests tended to take one of two forms: they were either aimed at specific local abuses, or grew into passionate, symbolic outbursts against a society they did not fully comprehend. This perception leads Le Roy Ladurie to contrast the revolts of the fifteenth and sixteenth centuries with what he regards as the national revolutionary movements of the Enlightenment:

[T]he rebels who rose up against different kinds of oppression did not always adopt a line of conduct that was – according to our own criteria – perfectly rational and capable of putting an end to their suffering. For a very long time they confined themselves to fighting the tax collector, whereas the real source of their difficulties lay in the social organisation itself and was much more general... The eighteenth century of the philosophers, whose activities would eventually prepare the way for the reception of political programmes from across the channel, still lay ahead.[39]

---

[38] *Ibid.*, p.300.   [39] *Ibid.*

Instead,

[T]raditional society at the end of our period, as far as the popular classes
are concerned, seems to have been characterised by a double series of
frustrations and deficiencies which mutually reinforced and conditioned
one another... The economy stagnated, society remained intractable, and
population – following its early triumphs – retreated, because society,
population and the economy lacked the progressive technology of true
growth. But they also lacked – at least as yet and at least to a sufficient
degree among the ruling classes and among the people – the conscience,
the culture, the morals, the politics, the education, the reformist spirit
and the unfettered longing for success which would have stimulated
technological initiative and the spirit of enterprise and permitted an
economic 'take off'.[40]

This teleological approach, which presents revolutions of the
sixteenth century as failed attempts to realise the political programmes of the Enlightenment, runs through Le Roy Ladurie's
work, and informs his attitude to specific classes of phenomena.
It is particularly noticeable in his discussion of what he regards
as 'irrational' protest movements, such as those associated with
witchcraft and satanism, and for our purposes these are of special
interest since they highlight the strategy used by the members of
the *Annales* school to explain individual beliefs and actions.

In *The Peasants of Languedoc*, satanism, witchcraft and possession
are consistently treated as aberrant social practices. They are seen
as the 'primitive' side of the peasant consciousness[41] and are
contrasted with 'the progress of Enlightenment' implied by the
Reformation.[42] In charting them, Le Roy Ladurie frequently uses
the device (a favourite of his) of describing them as infectious
diseases, and, indeed, relies on a whole range of similar metaphors.
'Beginning in 1850...the whole chain of bewitched mountains
began to stir once more, the chimneys of these great factories of
mass delirium started to smoke, and lines of force of demonic
influence spread from the Pyrenees to the Jura across the *langue
d'oc*-speaking heights of the Massif Central.'[43] In these 'frenzied
uprisings' 'the peasant consciousness suddenly broke loose from
its moorings, fell prey to ancient deliriums, and abandoned itself
to all its demons. In default of a veritable liberation it embarked
on the adventure of a satanic revolt.'[44] This way of thinking about

[40] *Ibid.*, p.302.   [41] *Ibid.*, p.202.   [42] *Ibid.*, p.206.
[43] *Ibid.*, p.205.   [44] *Ibid.*, p.208.

witchcraft and possession as manifestations of conscious and unconscious psychological states puts them in a particular light. Some questions seem obvious and others peculiar. Le Roy Ladurie himself characterises peasant witchcraft as expressing the frustration, anxiety and fear of people who were 'disillusioned with ideologies of urban origin, brutalised after 1560 by war, and haunted by the spectres of misery and death – and often by fears of sexual failure'.[45] He therefore pays attention to some of its most spectacular and to our eyes irrational forms, such as a widespread castration complex and symbolic inversion. And possession by the Holy Spirit, which was common among the Camisards, is put in the same light: riven by sexual frustration and guilt, this group suffered from mass hysteria in the form of fits and prophecies.

These explanations are fascinating in themselves, but nevertheless incorporate a certain bias. For witchcraft as exemplified by a fear of castration, and the Camisard revolt as exemplified by hysterical symptoms, are seen as irrational practices. They are fallings away from reason beyond conscious control, which require to be explained by an appeal to the unconscious.

In the course of his study Le Roy Ladurie thus employs two kinds of explanation. On the one hand, his book contains accounts of various structural constraints such as population size, wage levels, the sort of crops that could be grown, and so forth. Changes in these factors affect social organisation so that, to take a simple example, a greater number of people and a more or less constant amount of fertile land combined to reduce the size of holdings, which were divided among family members. This answer to the problem of overcrowding is not thought to need any further explanation because it is assumed to be the rational course of action: people saw that it was the only feasible thing to do, and acted accordingly. In this case individual beliefs and actions – the stuff of *événements* – are thus treated as an unproblematic response to structural variations.[46] On the other hand, Le Roy Ladurie employs a second sort of explanation to account for what he regards as *ir*rational beliefs and behaviour. Practices such as witchcraft are treated as the outcome of structural features, filtered

---

[45] *Ibid.*, p.207.

[46] See also Ladurie, *The Peasants of Languedoc*, pp.35–6. Another interesting and theoretically sophisticated example of this holist approach is provided by Theda Skocpol, *States and Social Revolutions* (Cambridge, 1979). For a critical discussion of her stance see John Dunn, 'Understanding Revolutions'.

through the unconscious, and manifested in uncontrolled expressions of fear, guilt or frustration. So between them, the two sorts of explanation treat beliefs and actions as either rational or unconscious responses to structures.

The fact that Le Roy Ladurie takes this dual approach is, I think, unsurprising, and derives from the problem of relating *structures* to individual beliefs and actions. We saw earlier on that Braudel, faced with the need to explain particular *événements*, resorts to a disorderly assortment of intentional explanations. Although Le Roy Ladurie's approach is less haphazard, he too switches back and forth between structural explanations that assume the rationality of individual agents, and those that appeal to the psychology of the unconscious. The abruptness of these transitions is partly concealed by the categories imposed on the data: by the assumption, for example, that rebellion in pursuit of economic gain is rational, whereas a belief in witchcraft is irrational and escapist. The fact that peasants seized opportunities to enrich themselves is put down to sheer good sense, an unproblematic response to structural changes, while the conviction that the Camisard prophets and prophetesses spoke with the voice of the Holy Spirit is regarded as obviously serving some psychological function. To this extent Le Roy Ladurie simply foists off our own values on the peasants of Languedoc, and exploits the prejudices of his readers about what does, and does not, need explaining.

Le Roy Ladurie therefore offers explanations in which an appeal to structural constraints is complemented either by an unexamined presumption of individual rationality or by an equally unexamined conception of the unconscious. But because the connections between these diverse types of explanation are not analysed, they do not throw any more light on the idea that holism and individualism answer to distinct explanatory interests. We still have to ask how these are related, and how they function.

Le Roy Ladurie's assumption of rationality, unanalysed though it is, is used to bring the interests of holism and individualism in line. The holist is enlightened by an account of the factors constraining people's actions. The individualist interest is served by the assumption that people see the constraints as binding them and act accordingly. Since there is no suggestion that their perception of their own situations may itself be explicable in holist terms, the two accounts are distinct, but are also complementary;

the conceptual space occupied by agents reflects the constraints under which they labour.

Such a harmonious union between holism and individualism may sometimes be achieved. But it may also be an uneasy truce, which can only be sustained as long as certain questions are not asked. Once we enquire, for example, what range of options are available to individual agents, or why they make the particular choices they do, the unsettled differences between the two views begin to emerge. Individualists who concede too much give up the very explanations which, from their perspective, make the phenomena intelligible. And holists who allow the individual agent too much ground leave their interest unsatisfied.[47] Frequently, therefore, their explanations will not fit together into a single picture.

This tension is interestingly brought out by Miller, when he argues that even if holist and individualist stories can both be told, the latter lacks any explanatory force without the counterfactual backing characteristic of holism. He elaborates the claim with the help of an example:

The change from carbon steel to stainless steel as the main material for knives would normally be explained as bound to happen, due to the greater capacity of stainless steel to keep its edge, together with the great reduction in the cost of stainless steel, as a result of technological advances in the 1920's. It is possible, in this case, to give a wholly individualistic description of the causes of the change, describing the episodes in which individual cutlery executives made actual decisions to switch production to stainless steel. But if this particular causal chain had not existed, stainless steel would still have replaced carbon steel as the main material for knives. Suppose that the executives in question had not formed beliefs to the effect that the material basis of knife production should be changed. Other people would have been smart enough to

[47] This conception of interests goes beyond the Weberean notion of a 'use-interest' distinct from an explanatory account. See A. Sen, 'Accounts, Actions and Values: The Objectivity of Social Science' in C. Lloyd ed. *Social Theory and Political Practice* (Oxford, 1983) pp.87–107. Concessive holism suggests a way of overcoming the limitations of the so-called 'strong programme' (see Barry Barnes, *Scientific Knowledge and Sociological Theory* (London, 1974) ch. 11, and David Bloor, *Knowledge and Social Imagery* (London, 1976)) and also offers an explanation of the blank disagreement between advocates of the programme and those who oppose it. See M. Hesse, 'Theory and Value in the Social Sciences' in C. Hookway and P. Pettit eds. *Action and Interpretation* (Cambridge, 1978) pp.1–16; M. Hollis, 'The Social Destruction of Reality' in M. Hollis and S. Lukes, eds. *Rationality and Relativism* (Oxford, 1983) pp.67–86.

perceive the implications of the technological advances and to use this perception either to drive those executives out of office or to drive their companies out of the market. That Mr Jones formed the belief 'We ought to switch to stainless'...does not explain why stainless steel was bound to replace carbon steel...For had [he] not formed [this] belief, the industrial capitalist system of production would, as it were, spontaneously correct for their stupidity.

Here again, the social scientist's interest in explaining what is bound to happen is so great, that the individualist saga fails to provide a social scientific explanation of why something happened.[48]

Miller's argument in this passage raises a number of issues. First, and parenthetically, it serves to remind us that the difference between the interests underlying individualism and holism is not merely the difference between showing why something happened to happen and why it had to happen, and thus between descriptive and counterfactual forms of explanation. In addition, as we saw in Chapter III, it concerns the *kind* of factor which makes the relevant counterfactual claims true. Thus the view that stainless steel knives would have replaced carbon steel ones even if individual industrialists had acted differently is justified by appealing to the competition inherent in capitalist production. This way of showing why a phenomenon is likely to occur by citing some *social* factor is what is characteristic of, and essential to, our interest in holist explanation. But Miller's analysis of his example also invites us to consider in more detail how this is related to an individualist interest. For when he spells out his conclusion, it appears to amount to the claim that, since people are not in general stupid, most cutlery executives would have seen the advantages of changing to stainless steel.[49] On the whole people can be expected to have 'seen the facts' and assessed the evidence correctly, and it is this generalisation that guarantees the truth of the counterfactual in question. However, this judgment embodies a conception of individual rationality which is quite compatible with the individualist case, and thus obscures the point that holist explanations, while they *may* be complemented by individualist ones, need not be.

This feature of holism is brought out more clearly by G. A. Cohen who, in the course of discussing Marx's theory of history,

[48] Miller, 'Methodological Individualism and Social Explanation' pp.410–11.
[49] *Ibid.*, p.411.

gives an account of the kind of functionalism implicit in Miller's examples. To take one of his cases, there are some industries in which an increase in the size of factories or workshops reduces the cost of production.[50] We may explain the fact that the production units of a particular industry have grown larger over a period of time by appealing to the economies this yields, and in doing so claim that a cause (increase in scale) occurred because of its propensity to have a certain effect (economies of scale). Now, this example is analogous to the holist explanations proposed by Miller. In the first case we considered, a belief shared by leading industrialists (their tendency to identify the interests of their own class with those of their country) was attributed to the system of education, the media and so on. We could now go on to attempt to explain the character of these institutions by citing their effect on leading capitalists – they are as they are partly because they encourage a belief which is functional in relation to the system as a whole. Similarly, in Miller's second example, the shift by particular cutlery businesses from carbon to stainless steel is explained by its tendency to make their enterprises more competitive. And the same change throughout the industry can be accounted for by the functional fact that only those firms which made this change would have survived the competition.

Although these instances serve to illustrate the character of holist explanation, and to show how it can occur without any individualist counterpart, they may be too isolated to be persuasive. It is important to remember, however, that explanations of this type are also the stock-in-trade of such subjects as demography and criminology, which aim to establish generalisations relating social factors to human behaviour. In these fields, too, we are sometimes able to identify social phenomena such as an increase in population size, which we can *use* to explain other phenomena, while at the same time being unable to identify any corresponding regularities in the behaviour or attitudes of individual agents. It is true that, in all these cases, individualists will deny that we have arrived at an explanation. We have discovered a connection, they will say, on the basis of which we can predict. But until we have found out why the generalisation holds by complementing it with an account of the actions and attitudes of individuals, we will not have explained what is going on. It is open to holists, however,

[50] G. A. Cohen, *Karl Marx's Theory of History: A Defense* (Princeton, 1978) p.280.

to resist this conclusion, and Cohen distinguishes two ways in which they can do so. First, although it may be true that functional explanations of the kind he discusses remain incomplete until we understand the mechanisms which sustain them, they may nevertheless be explanatory. The justification for this view is partly pragmatic; as Cohen puts it, 'it would be a mistake to refrain from taking those explanatory steps which are open to us, just because we should prefer to go farther than our current knowledge permits'.[51] But a willingness to accept claims about the functional relations between the properties of social ·wholes and those of individuals as explanatory also stems from a sympathy with the underlying interest of holism. Individualists who deny that these claims explain anything at all are, in effect, simply reasserting the hegemony of the interest from which individualism draws its life, while holists are pursuing their own concern with the constraining power of society.

Exponents of the two approaches are therefore at odds with one another.[52] But they are nevertheless able to agree that it is sometimes possible to elaborate functional relations of the sort we have considered. For the individualist, the way to do this is clear: a complementary individualist story must be told. But as Cohen suggests, echoing Miller's point, there are also cases where an individualist account adds nothing to the explanation. This comes out most clearly in Cohen's own example of the connection between increases and economies of scale within a competitive economy. As we saw earlier, the fact that the producing units of an industry increase in size over a number of years may be explained by the functional relation between their size and the cost of production. Larger firms, by virtue of having expanded, are better able to survive in a competitive market. If we ask in this type of case *why* businesses expanded, there may sometimes by no systematic explanation to be given.[53] Some firms may have grown in an unplanned, unforeseen manner, others may have expanded in order to acquire greater prestige and so on. Suppose that, in the first case, we can give a detailed account of how expansion occurred, and in the second can recount the calculations and decisions of the firm's executives. These histories, taken singly or

[51] *Ibid.*, p.286.
[52] See the debate between Elster, Cohen *et al* in *Theory and Society* 11 (1982).
[53] G. A. Cohen, *Karl Marx's Theory of History* pp.287–8.

together, do not seem to tell us what we want to know, since they do not help us to understand why cutlery firms *in general* increased in size. Rather, they reveal what Cohen calls a Darwinian mechanism: in a climate of scarcity, competition will select for firms that are efficient, whatever the reasons for their efficiency.[54]

Cases such as those discussed by Miller and Cohen provide evidence for the claim that holist explanations are sometimes autonomous in the sense that no individualist account serves to supplement them. In this chapter, I have sought to defend this concessive holist view by drawing attention to the explanatory interest underlying it. Adopting this pragmatic approach, I have thus sought to justify the main general conclusion to which my whole argument has been directed: that the way to heal the rift between holism and individualism is to recognise that concessive holism offers a superior approach to the business of social explanation.

[54] *Ibid.*

Conclusion

Holist explanations are widely acknowledged to play a vital part in our understanding of the social world. Before their status can be assured, however, the challenge traditionally posed by individualism must be overcome, and the entrenched opposition between the two views transcended. In the course of this book I have argued that, despite its unyielding appearance, the problem of holism can indeed be resolved: the stalemate between individualists and holists stems from their failure to perceive a number of dimensions which, once they are made explicit, point toward a solution.

The aim, then, has been to see the problem afresh, and a first reformulation of it was offered in Chapter III. I claimed there that holists and individualists are not in fact disagreeing principally over the issue of reduction as has generally been supposed. They are more fundamentally divided by their disparate conceptions of the human individual – a fact which lies at the heart of their views of explanation. Crucial to individualism is the conviction that people are agents who determine the course of events both by choosing between existing options, and by creating the options themselves. Good explanations must accordingly respect this vision by giving pride of place to the individual beliefs and purposes which shape the social world. Holists, on the contrary, are concerned to understand the ways in which individuals are constrained by their social environments and argue that the best explanations are informed by this standpoint. The main difference between the two approaches is thus their commitment to discrete ranges of causal factors – to the beliefs, actions and intentions of individuals on the one hand, to the constraining properties of social wholes on the other.

Having identified this implicit feature of the debate in Part I, I went on in Part II to ask how the holist approach has fared: how powerful and wide-ranging are the holist explanations currently proposed by social scientists? I argued in Chapters IV and V that the ambition of absolute holism to supplant individualism completely is too strong to be realised. We cannot now implement the whole of that programme and must look for a more concessive approach, capable of accommodating the competing strengths of individualism. Holists therefore face the pressing task of effecting a compromise: they must somehow overcome the opposition between their own view of the individual and that held by individualists in order to arrive at a coherent theory.

In Chapter VI I suggested a way in which this can be achieved. Since the conflict between holism and individualism runs so deep, the two modes of explanation cannot be simply amalgamated, and no metaphysical resolution is forthcoming. Each approach reflects, however, a particular kind of concern with social explanation, and the two views are most fruitfully regarded as the outcomes of distinct explanatory interests. These motivate the separate preoccupations of holists and individualists, each with a characteristic type of question, and account for the fact that they are satisfied by different sorts of answers. For the individualist, the central task is to understand individuals as agents, and thus as far as possible to understand the social world as the outcome of options and choices taken and made by particular actors. Holists, by contrast, have a different interest. Instead of cherishing a liberal conception of the individual, they direct their attention to the social regularities which control classes of people. By isolating these features, they argue, we can arrive at explanations which either elucidate the relations between large-scale social phenomena, or relate these to individual actions and attitudes.

Once we recognise that holists and individualists are pursuing separate interests, it becomes clear that we need a scheme which will accommodate them both, and I have argued that the *Annales* school offers us the seeds of such an approach. Their categories of *structure* and *événement* (though not designed for these purposes, and thus serving them only crudely), allow a place for both holist and individualist explanations without requiring that they should always fit neatly together. The charge that Braudel fails to relate *événements* to *structures* is, as we saw, amply justified; but it comes to seem less destructive once we think of holists and individualists as engaged in separate projects. This point comes out most explicitly in Le Roy Ladurie's work on Languedoc, where the explanations he offers have two kinds of appeal. From a holist perspective it is Le Roy Ladurie's analysis of the impact of structural factors which is illuminating, whereas, as far as individualists are concerned, it is his implicit assumption of instrumental rationality which does the real explanatory work. In some of the cases he deals with these interests supplement one another; but they nevertheless remain distinct.

It may be objected that my argument defines individualism too narrowly; for rather than contrasting the properties of individuals as such with those of social wholes, I have focussed on a particular range of traits, and in doing so may be said to have neglected properties to which the individualist can legitimately appeal. But this omission is a consequence of my claim that individualism is fundamentally designed to sustain a conception of individuals as agents. The resulting emphasis on their purposive properties – on their choices, decisions, intentions, actions and beliefs – is, as I have argued, what divides individualists from holists. This means that, while we can acknowledge the existence of other kinds of individual properties, they are relatively incidental to the problem of holism. If humans were not perceived as capable of autonomous action, the question of how we should explain the social world would be transformed, in a way that – as Althusser's work reveals – it is hard to imagine. Perhaps we might then be concerned with issues such as the relative merits of explanations that appeal to behavioural drives and those that appeal to ideological structures; but the problem of holism as we now know it would simply not exist. My account of individualism therefore emphasises a set of features, central to this problem, which also define a distinctively individualist interest in explanation.

To invoke the idea of an interest, as I have done, to resolve the dispute between holists and individualists is to allow that the canons of explanation in the social sciences are both pragmatic and normative. Holists and individualists may both be said to have an overarching interest in understanding the mechanisms which operate in the social world, but beneath this unifying umbrella their eyes are fixed on different features on the landscape, and their respective theories are to be judged in relation to the tasks they set themselves. A theory which provides wide-ranging holist explanations, for example, will be successful, not in the light of any general conception of what it is to explain things, but in the light of the much more limited interest guiding holism. So in this sense the approach is a pragmatic one, which bears on the here and now rather than on eternity.[1] At the same time, to formulate the problem in terms of interests, as I have done, is to focus attention on the moral priorities embedded in holism and individualism. To pursue one of these modes of explanation is inevitably to adopt a strongly normative picture of what the social world is like and why we should bother with it. So the claim that there can be more than one legitimate interest brings with it the corollary that explanation can be underpinned by more than one set of norms. Anyone who follows this approach wholeheartedly must therefore be prepared for eclectic results: on the one hand theories inspired by a commitment to a moral ideal of autonomy and individual responsibility; on the other, work which aims to subvert that very view.

This moral variety may seem a high price to pay for the resolution of the problem of holism. But it is a central implication of the argument I have presented that this price will have to be paid. This being so, it is all the more important to end by underlining what I take to be gained by the acceptance of my proposal that concessive holism should be adopted as the most fruitful approach to social explanation. The argument I have advanced aims to shake a widespread and intuitive adherence to individualism by putting it on a par with its holist rival. As we have seen, individualists faced with holist explanations commonly ask for more. All they have been offered, they feel, is a gesture toward an explanation – a menu of dishes whose aromas and flavours have yet to be tried. They are inclined to forget that holists, when served individualist explanations, are assailed by a like hunger. To satisfy their interests they too need to know more, and in the meantime suffer the same sense of incompleteness. This insensitivity on the part of individualists is due, as I have argued, both to a failure of imagination and to moral nervousness; they are alarmed by an approach which, as one commentator puts it, sees 'human individuality as the fantasy of a creature constitutionally unable to apprehend its rigidly social location'.[2] But to attack holism on

---

[1] R. Rorty, *Philosophy and the Mirror of Nature.*

[2] John Dunn, 'Social Theory, Social Understanding and Political Action' in C. Lloyd ed. *Social Theory and Political Practice* p.119.

these grounds is, as I have sought to show, merely to reassert the alleged hegemony of the individualist interest. Why this should be our only or even our overriding concern remains as opaque as ever. In effect it is merely to restate the fact that the intuitions that sustain the case for individualism in explanation are largely *our* intuitions. It has been the main argument of this book, however, that this objection ought not to be allowed to have the last word.

Bibliography of works cited in the text

Althusser, L., *For Marx*, trans. B. Brewster (London, 1965)
Lenin, Philosophy and Other Essays, trans. B. Brewster (London, 1971)
Politics and History, trans. B. Brewster (London, 1972)
Réponse à John Lewis (Paris, 1973)
Essays in Self Criticism, trans. G. Locke (London, 1976)
Althusser, L. and Balibar, E., *Reading Capital*, trans. B. Brewster (London, 1970)
Anderson, P., *Arguments within English Marxism* (London, 1980)
Anscombe, E., *Intention* (Oxford, 1957)
Ashton, T. S., *The Industrial Revolution* (London, 1948)
Austin, J. L., 'A Plea for Excuses' in *Philosophical Papers* (Oxford, 1961)
Balibar, E., 'The Basic Concepts of Historical Materialism' in L. Althusser and E. Balibar, *Reading Capital*, trans. B. Brewster (London, 1970)
Barnes, B., *Scientific Knowledge and Sociological Theory* (London, 1974); *Interests and the Growth of Knowledge* (London, 1977).
Baron, W., Nagel, E. and Pinson, K., eds., *Freedom and Reason* (Glencoe, 1951)
Beales, D., *History and Biography* (Cambridge, 1981)
Benton, T., *Philosophical Foundations of the Three Sociologies* (London, 1977)
Berger, J. and Offe, C. 'Functionalism and Rational Choice', *Theory and Society* 11 (1982) pp.521–6
Bergmann, G., 'Holism, Historicism and Emergence', *Philosophy of Science* 4 (1944) pp.209–21
Berlin, I., *Four Essays on Liberty* (Oxford, 1969)
Bhaskar, R., *The Possibility of Naturalism* (Brighton, 1979)
Block, W., 'On Nozick's "On Austrian Methodology"', *Inquiry* 23 (1980) pp.397–444
Bloor, D., *Knowledge and Social Imagery* (London, 1976)
Bradley, F. H. *Ethical Studies* 1st edn (London, 1876)
Braudel, F., 'Pour ou contre une politicologie scientifique' *Annales: Économies, sociétés, civilisations* 18 (1963)
The Mediterranean and the Mediterranean World in the Age of Philip II 2 vols., trans. S. Reynolds (London, 1972)

'History and the Social Sciences' in P. Burke, ed. *Economy and Society in Early Modern Europe* (London, 1972)

Bridgstock, M. and Hyland, M., 'The Nature of Individualist Explanation: A Further Analysis of Reduction', *Philosophy of the Social Sciences* 8 (1978) pp.265–9

'Reductionism: Comments on Some Recent Work', *Philosophy of the Social Sciences* 4 (1974) pp.197–200

Brodbeck, M., 'Methodological Individualism: Definition and Reduction' in J. O'Neill ed., *Modes of Individualism and Collectivism* (London, 1973) pp.277–86

Brown, R., *Rules and Laws in Sociology* (London, 1973)

Burke, P., 'Reflections on the Historical Revolution in France: the Annales School and British Social History', *Review* 1 (1978) pp.147–56

Caplan, J. 'Theories of Fascism: Nicos Poulantzas as Historian', *History Workshop* 3 (1977) pp.83–100

Carnap, R., *The Unity of Science* (London, 1934)

'Logical Foundations of the Unity of Science' in O. Neurath, R. Carnap, C. Morris, eds., *International Encyclopaedia of Unified Science* vol. 1 (Chicago, 1955)

'The Old and the New Logic' in A. J. Ayer ed., *Logical Positivism* (New York, 1959)

Clarke, S., 'Marxism, Sociology and Poulantzas' Theory of the State', *Capital and Class* 2 (1977) pp.1–31

Cohen, G. A., *Karl Marx's Theory of History: A Defense* (Princeton, 1978)

'Reply to Elster on Marxism, Functionalism, and Game Theory' in *Theory and Society* 11 (1982) pp.483–95

Coleman, J., 'Collective Decision and Collective Action' in P. Laslett, W. G. Runciman, Q. Skinner, eds., *Philosophy, Politics and Society* 4th series (Oxford, 1972) p.208

Power and the Structure of Society (New York, 1974)

Connell, R. W., 'A Critique of the Althusserean Approach to Class' in *Theory and Society* 8 (1979) pp.303–45

Connolly, W. E., *Appearance and Reality in Politics* (Cambridge, 1981)

Copp, D., 'Collective Actions and Secondary Actions', *American Philosophical Quarterly* 16 (1979) pp.177–86;

'Hobbes on Artificial Persons and Collective Action', *Philosophical Review* 89 (1980) pp.579–606.

Crouzet, F., 'England and France in the Eighteenth Century: A Comparative Analaysis of Two Economic Growths' in R. M. Hartwell, ed., *The Causes of the Industrial Revolution in England* (London, 1967)

Davidson, D., 'Actions, Reasons and Causes' in A. R. White, ed., *The Philosophy of Action* (Oxford, 1968) pp.79–94

'Freedom to Act' in T. Honderich ed. *Essays on Freedom of Action* (London, 1973)

Dawe, A., 'The Two Sociologies', *British Journal of Sociology* 21 (1970) p.207

Dray, W., *Laws and Explanation in History* (London, 1957)

Dreyfus, H., 'Holism and Hermeneutics', *The Review of Metaphysics* 34 (1980) pp.3–23

Dummett, M., 'What is a Theory of Meaning?' (I) in S. Guttenplan ed. *Mind and Language* (Oxford, 1975) pp.97–138

'What is a Theory of Meaning?' (II) in G. Evans and J. McDowell eds, *Truth and Meaning* (Oxford, 1976)

Dunn, J., 'Understanding Revolutions', *Ethics* 92 (1982) pp.299–315

'Social Theory, Social Understanding and Political Action' in C. Lloyd ed., *Social Theory and Political Practice* (Oxford, 1983) pp.109–35

Eberle, R., Kaplan, D. and Montague, R., 'Hempel and Oppenheim on Explanation', *Philosophy of Science* 28 (1961) pp.418–28

Elster, J., *Logic and Society* (New York, 1978)

'Marxism, Functionalism and Game Theory: The Case for Methodological Individualism', *Theory and Society* 11 (1982) pp.453–82

Feinberg, J., 'Action and Responsibility' in A. R. White ed., *The Philosophy of Action* (Oxford, 1968)

Feyerabend, P. K., 'Explanation, Reduction and Empiricism' in H. Feigl and G. Maxwell eds., *Scientific Explanation, Space and Time. Minnesota Studies in the Philosophy of Science* vol. III (Minneapolis, 1962)

'Reply to Criticism' in R. S. Cohen and M. W. Wartofsky eds., *Boston Studies in the Philosophy of Science* Vol. II (Boston, 1965)

'Problems of Empiricism' in R. G. Colodny ed., *Beyond the Edge of Certainty* (Englewood Cliffs, 1965)

Against Method (London, 1978)

Fodor, J. A., *The Language of Thought* (Hassocks, 1976)

Forster, R., 'The Achievements of the Annales School', *Journal of Economic History* 38 (1978) pp.58–76

Frankfurt, H., 'Freedom of the Will and the Concept of a Person', *Journal of Philosophy* 68 (1971) pp.5–20

French, P., 'The Corporation as a Moral Person', *American Philosophical Quarterly* 16 (1979) pp.207–15

'Crowds and Corporations', *American Philosophical Quarterly* 19 (1982) pp.271–77

Garnett, A., 'Scientific Method and the Concept of Emergence', *Journal of Philosophy* 39 (1942) pp.477–86

Gellner, E., 'Explanation in History' in J. O'Neill ed., *Modes of Individualism and Collectivism* (London, 1973) pp.248–63

Giddens, A., *Central Problems in Social Theory: Action, Structure and Contradiction in Social Analysis* (London, 1979)

A Contemporary Critique of Historical Materialism (London, 1981)

Goldstein, L. J., 'Two Theses of Methodological Individualism' in J. O'Neill ed., *Modes of Individualism and Collectivism* (London, 1973) pp.277–86

Goodman, N., *Ways of Worldmaking* (Hassocks, 1978)

Habermas, J. *Knowledge and Human Interests*, trans. J. Shapiro (Boston, 1971)

Hagen, E., 'On the Theory of Social Change' in T. Burns and S. Saul eds., *Social Theory and Economic Change* (London, 1967)

Hall, J., 'The Time of History and the History of Times', *History and Theory* 19 (1980) pp.113–31

Hall, S., 'Nicos Poulantzas: State, Power, Socialism', *New Left Review* 119 (1980) pp.60–9

Hanson, N. R., *Patterns of Discovery* (Cambridge, 1958)

Hart, H. L. A., 'The Ascription of Responsibility and Rights', *Proceedings of the Aristotelian Society* (1948–9) pp.171–94

Hart, H. L. A. and Honoré, A., *Causation and the Law* (Oxford, 1959).

Hayek, F. A., *The Counter-Revolution of Science* (New York, 1964)

Held, V., 'Can a Random Collection of Individuals be Morally Responsible?', *Journal of Philosophy* 67 (1970) pp.471–81

Heller, A., 'Individual and Community', *Social Praxis* 1 (1973) pp.11–22

Hempel, C., 'Implications of Carnap's work for the Philosophy of Science' in P. A. Schilpp, ed., *The Philosophy of Rudolf Carnap* (La Salle, Illinois, 1963) pp.685–709

Aspects of Scientific Explanation (New York, 1965)

The Philosophy of the Natural Sciences (Englewood Cliffs, 1966)

'Reduction: Ontological and Linguistic Facets' in S. Morgenbesser, P. Suppes, M. White, eds. in *Philosophy, Science and Method* (New York, 1969)

Henle, P., 'The Status of Emergence', *Journal of Philosophy* 39 (1942) pp.486–93

Hesse, M., *The Structure of Scientific Inference* (London, 1974)

'Theory and Value in the Social Sciences' in C. Hookway and P. Pettit eds., *Action and Interpretation* (Cambridge, 1978)

Hollis, M., *Models of Man* (Cambridge, 1977)

'The Social Destruction of Reality' in M. Hollis and S. Lukes eds., *Rationality and Relativism* (Oxford, 1983)

Hull, D., *The Philosophy of Biological Science* (Englewood Cliffs, 1974)

Hutton, P., 'The History of Mentalities: The New Map of Cultural History', *History and Theory* 20 (1981) pp.237–59

Joll, J., 'Politicians and the Freedom to Choose' in A. Ryan ed., *The Idea of Freedom* (Oxford, 1979)

Kenny, A., *Action, Emotion and Will* (London, 1963)

Kuhn, T., *The Structure of Scientific Revolutions* (Chicago, 1962)

Laclau, E., *Politics and Ideology in Marxist Theory* (London, 1977)

Ladurie, E. Le Roy, *Times of Feast, Times of Famine*, trans. B. Bray (London, 1972)

The Peasants of Languedoc, trans. J. Day (Chicago, 1974)

Leplin, E. ed. *Essays on Scientific Realism* (Notre Dame, 1983)

Lessnoff, M., *The Structure of Social Science* (London, 1975)

Lugg, A., 'Putnam on Reductionism', *Cognition* 3 (1973–4) pp.289–93

Lukes, S., *Individualism* (Oxford, 1973)

Essays in Social Theory (London, 1977)

'Elster on Counterfactuals', *Inquiry* 23 (1980) pp.145–55

Macdonald, G. and Pettit, P., *Semantics and Social Science* (London, 1981)

Mandelbaum, M., 'Societal Facts' in J. O'Neill ed., *Modes of Individualism and Collectivism* (London, 1973) pp.221–34

Martin, M., 'Reduction and Typical Individuals Again', *Philosophy of the Social Sciences* 5 (1975) pp.307–8

Marx, K., *Introduction to the Grundrisse*, trans. M. Nicolaus (Harmondsworth, 1973)

Capital vol. 1, trans. S. Moore and E. Aveling (London, 1954)

Mathias, P., *The First Industrial Nation* (London, 1969)

Maull, N., 'Unifying Science Without Reduction', *Studies in the History and Philosophy of Science* 8 (1977) pp.143–62

Melden, I., *Free Action* (London, 1961)

Mellor, D. H., 'The Reduction of Society', *Philosophy* 57 (1982) pp.51–75

Mennell, S., *Sociological Theory: Uses and Unities* 2nd edn (Walton-on-Thames, 1980)

Miliband, R., 'Poulantzas and the Capitalist State', *New Left Review* 82 (1973) pp.83–92

Marxism and Politics (Oxford, 1977)

Miller, R., 'Methodological Individualism and Social Explanation', *Philosophy of Science* 45 (1978) pp.387–414

Nagel, E., *The Structure of Science* (London, 1961)

Nagel, T., 'Subjective and Objective' in *Mortal Questions* (Cambridge, 1979)

Needham, J., *Time: The Refreshing River* (London, 1943)

Newton-Smith, W. H., *The Rationality of Science* (London, 1981)

Nickles, T., 'Two Concepts of Intertheoretic Reduction', *Journal of Philosophy* 70 (1973) pp.181–201

Nozick, R., 'On Austrian Methodology', *Synthese* 36 (1977) pp.353–92

Offe, C. and Ronge, V., 'Theses on the Theory of the State', *New German Critique* 6 (1975) pp.139–47

Olin Wright, E., *Class, Crisis and the State* (London, 1978)

Olson, M., *The Logic of Collective Action* (Cambridge, Mass., 1971)

O'Neill, J. ed., *Modes of Individualism and Collectivism* (London, 1973)

Opp, Karl-Dieter, 'Group Size, Emergence and Composition Laws: Are There Macroscopic Theories *sui generis?*', *The Philosophy of the Social Sciences* 9 (1979) pp.445–55

Peacocke, C., *Holistic Explanation* (Oxford, 1979)

Pettit, P., *Judging Justice* (London, 1980)

Plekhanov, G. V., 'The Role of the Individual in History' in J. Allen ed. *Fundamental Problems of Marxism* (London, 1969)

Popper, K., *The Open Society and its Enemies* 2 vols. (London, 1946) *The Poverty of Historicism* (London, 1957)

Poulantzas, N., *Political Power and Social Classes*, trans. Timothy O'Hagan (London, 1975)
Fascism and Dictatorship, trans. J. White (London, 1974)
Classes in Contemporary Capitalism, trans. D. Fernbach (London, 1975)
'Reply to Miliband and Laclau', *New Left Review* 95 (1976) p.82
'Towards a Democratic Socialism', *New Left Review* 109 (1978) pp.75–87

Pratt, V., *The Philosophy of the Social Sciences* (London, 1977)

Putnam, H., 'Reductionism and the Nature of Psychology', *Cognition* 2 (1972–3) pp.131–46
Meaning and the Moral Sciences (London, 1978)
'Three kinds of Scientific Realism', *Philosophical Quarterly* 32 (1982) pp.197–200

Quine, W. V. O., *From a Logical Point of View* (Cambridge, Mass., 1953)

Quinton, A., 'Social Objects', *Proceedings of the Aristotelian Society* 75 (1975–6) p.23

Rawls, J., 'Kantian Constructivism in Moral Theory', *Journal of Philosophy* 78 (1980) pp.515–35

Roemer, J., 'Methodological Individualism and Deductive Materialism', *Theory and Society* 11 (1982) pp.513–20

Rorty, R., *Philosophy and the Mirror of Nature* (Princeton, 1979)
'A Reply to Dreyfus and Taylor', *The Review of Metaphysics* 34 (1980) pp.39–46
'Method, Social Science and Social Hope' in *Consequences of Pragmatism* (Minneapolis, 1982)

Ruben, D. H., 'The Existence of Social Entities' in *Philosophical Quarterly* 32 (1982) pp.295–310

Runciman, W. G., *A Critique of Max Weber's Philosophy of the Social Sciences* (Cambridge, 1972)

Ryan, A., *The Philosophy of the Social Sciences* (London, 1970)

Schaffner, K., 'The Peripherality of Reduction in the Development of Molecular Biology', *Journal of the History of Biology* 7 (1964) pp.111–39

'The Watson-Crick Model and Reductionism', *British Journal of the Philosophy of Science* 20 (1969) pp.325–48

Scriven, M., 'Explanations, Predictions and Laws' in F. Feigl, and G. Maxwell eds. *Scientific Explanation, Space and Time, Minnesota Studies in the Philosophy of Science* vol. III (Minneapolis, 1962)

Sen, A., 'Accounts, Actions and Values: The Objectivity of Social Science' in C. Lloyd ed., *Social Theory and Political Practice* (Oxford, 1983) pp.87–107

Sklar, L., 'Types of Intertheoretic Reduction', *British Journal of the Philosophy of Science* 18 (1967) pp.109–24

Skocpol, T., *States and Social Revolutions* (Cambridge, 1979)

Smart, B., 'Foucault, Sociology and the Problem of Human Agency', *Theory and Society* 11 (1982) pp.121–42

Spector, M., *Concepts of Reduction in Physical Science* (Philadelphia, 1978)

Stoianovich, T., *French Historical Method: The Annales Paradigm* (Ithaca, 1976)

Strawson, P., 'Freedom and Resentment' in *Studies in the Philosophy of Thought and Action* (Oxford, 1968)

Taylor, C., 'Understanding in Human Science', *The Review of Metaphysics* 34 (1980) pp.25–38

Thompson, E. P., *The Poverty of Theory and Other Essays* (London, 1978)

Torrance, J., 'Methods and the Man', *Archives Européenes de Sociologie* 15 (1974) p.147

Trevor Roper, H. R., 'Ferdinand Braudel, the *Annales* and the Mediterranean', *Journal of Modern History* 44 (1972) pp.468–79

'History and Imagination' in H. Lloyd Jones, V. Pearl, B. Worden eds., *History and Imagination: Essays in Honour of H. R. Trevor Roper* (London, 1981)

Tribe, K., 'On the Production and Structuring of Scientific Knowledges', *Economy and Society* 2 (1973)

van Fraassen, B., *The Scientific Image* (Oxford, 1980)

von Mises, L., *Human Action: A Treatise on Economics* (London, 1949)

Watkins, J. W. N., 'Ideal Types and Historical Explanation' in J. O'Neill ed., *Modes of Individualism and Collectivism* (London, 1973) pp.143–65

'Methodological Individualism: A Reply' in J. O'Neill ed. *Modes of Individualism and Collectivism* (London, 1973) pp.179–84

'Historical Explanation in the Social Sciences' in J. O'Neill ed., *Modes of Individualism and Collectivism* (London, 1973) pp.166–78

Wiggins, D., 'Towards a Reasonable Libertarianism' in T. Honderich ed., *Essays on Freedom of Action* (London, 1973)

Wilson, C., 'The Entrepreneur in the Industrial Revolution in Britain', *History* (1957) pp.101–17.

Index

Index

189

Clarke, S., 118n
classes,
    Poulantzas' analysis of, 119, 120,
        124, 126, 131–4, 136
    hegemony of, 121
    and structures, 123, 124, 131
    positions of, 124, 125
    fractions of, 126, 127, 129, 131
    strata of, 126, 131
    dominance of, 126–9
class-consciousness, 62–4, 120
class interests, 120, 121–2, 124,
    126–8, 141, 142
class strategy, 124, 140–4
class struggle, 118, 122–32
classical political economy, 82, 84–7,
    89, 90
Cohen, G. A., 8n, 172, 173n, 174,
    175
Coleman, J., 47n
composition rules, 53
concessive holism, 9, 147, 148, 151–5
    scope of, 155–7, 165
    and Annales school, 158, 164–6,
        168
    strengths of, 171–9
conjunctures, 160–4, 169, 170
Connell, R. W., 123n
Connolly, W. E., 114, 115, 116
contradictions
    between practice, 93–7, 101, 125
    between structures, 123, 125
    in Poulantzas' theory, 136, 137
Copp, D., 47n
counterfactual argument, 134–6
    and structures, 138
    and class struggle, 139, 140–4
    and concessive holism, 147, 151,
        153–5, 164, 165, 171, 172
    and absolute holism, 130, 137, 138,
        148–50
Crouzet, F., 65

Davidson, D., 7n, 59n
Dawe, A., 58n
Descartes, R., 107
determinism, 66–72, 114
Dray, W., 26n
Dreyfus, H., 37n
Dummett, M., 5n
Dunn, J., 62n, 179

Eberle, R., 26n

economic determination 'in the last
    instance', 96, 98–101, 122, 123
economism, 122 133
Elster, J., 8n, 135n
emergence, 2n
empiricism, 4, 5
Engels, F., 122
epistemological breaks, 80, 83
événements, 160, 161, 164, 165
explanation
    functional, 173, 174
    of action, 7, 49–51, 57, 70–4, 102,
        147
    causal, see individualist
        explanation; individuals; holist
        explanation
    see also interests in explanation

facism, 118
Febvre, L., 158, 162
Feinberg, J., 7n
Feyerabend, P., 4n, 26n, 28, 29, 29n,
    31n
Fodor, J., 27
Foncault, 114
Forster, R., 157n
Frankfurt, H., 59n
French, P., 47n
Freud, 73

Galileo, 84
Garnett, A., 2n
Gellner, E., 44n
Giddens, A, 58n, 118n
Goldstein, L. J., 39n
Goodman, N., 5n
group predicates, 38, 40, 41, 45–50

Habermas, H., 156n
Hagen, E., 65n
Hall, J., 160n
Hall, S., 118n
Hanson, N. R., 24n
Hart, H. L. A., 7n
Hayek, F. A., 21n
Held, V., 47n
Heller, A., 47n
Hempel, C., 4n, 19n, 25n, 30n
Henle, P., 2n
hermeneutics, 82, 83
Hesse, M., 4n, 24n, 29, 171n
histoire totale, 159–61, 166
historical accidents, 60–2, 149–51

historicist analysis of state, 120, 122
history as a 'process without a
subject', 101–5
holism
of content, 2, 3, 5–9, 13, 58–64, 69
of form, 3–6, 45
see also problem of holism;
absolute holism; concessive
holism
holist explanation
and reduction, 6, 13–16, 20, 45
and causes of social phenomena,
6–7, 58–60, 65, 66, 69, 70, 70–5,
146, 147
Hollis, M., 58n, 171n
Honore, A., 7n
Hull, David, 27, 28, 31
human nature, 6
in individualism, 58, 59, 72, 73
in classical political economy,
85–90
in absolute holism, 114, 115
Hutton, P., 157n
Hyland, M., 14n, 15n, 39n

idealism, 82
ideological practice, 102–7, 111–17
ideological state apparatuses, 92,
111–13, 115, 116
ideology
and science, 83, 116–17
of the capitalist state, 128, 129
individual predicates, 23, 24, 38, 39,
50, 58
individualism
as accepted view, 8–9, 13, 53–4,
66
defences of, 22–3, 40–3, 45, 48–52
and anti-determinism, 60–8
normative foundations of, 7, 20,
55–60, 69–74, 178–180
motivation for, 156
see also logical positivism; reduction;
individuals
individualist explanation, 57–74,
173–9
and reduction, 15, 16, 25, 26,
40–3, 45, 49–53
Poulantzas' discussion of, 120
see also individualism; concessive
holism
individualist theories, 6, 38, 39, 40–3
individuals

as bearers of practices, 80, 86,
101–9, 116, 123
as agents, 57–64, 70–1, 74, 101–3,
109–12, 116, 176, 178
intentional properties of, 7, 40–2,
57–60, 63, 64, 70–2, 101, 102,
108, 113–14, 116, 120
causal powers of, 149–52, 57, 64
instances of totality, 122, 123, 132–3
political, 122, 123, 125
economic, 122, 123
ideological, 122
dominant, 122
interests in explanation, 9, 156–8,
163, 164, 170–8
internal relations, 3, 45

Joll, J., 62n

Kant, I., 73, 107
Kaplan, D., 26n
Kenny, A., 7n
Kuhn, T. S., 24n, 26n

Laclau, E., 130
Le Roy Ladurie, E., 158, 159, 161n,
164
explanations used by, 169–71, 178
Peasants of Languedoc, 164n, 166–9
legitimation, 100, 101, 112–16
Lenin, 93, 96, 97, 98, 101, 124, 125
Leplin, J., 5n
Lessnoff, M., 19n, 22
logical positivism, 16–18
and theory of meaning, 17, 21–4
see unification of science
longue durée, 160, 161, 162
Lugg, A., 34n
Lukes, S., 39n, 109, 110, 135n

Macdonald, G., 41n
Mandelbaum, M., 2n, 14n, 39n, 43,
44, 45
Mao Tse Tung, 96, 97
Martin, M., 39n
Marx, K., 62, 81–111 passim, 117,
122
on political economy, 84–90
materialism of, 88–101, 105
on the state, 119–20
theory of history of, 82, 84, 86,
172, 173
Capital, 83, 84, 99

62547